WELCOME
HOME

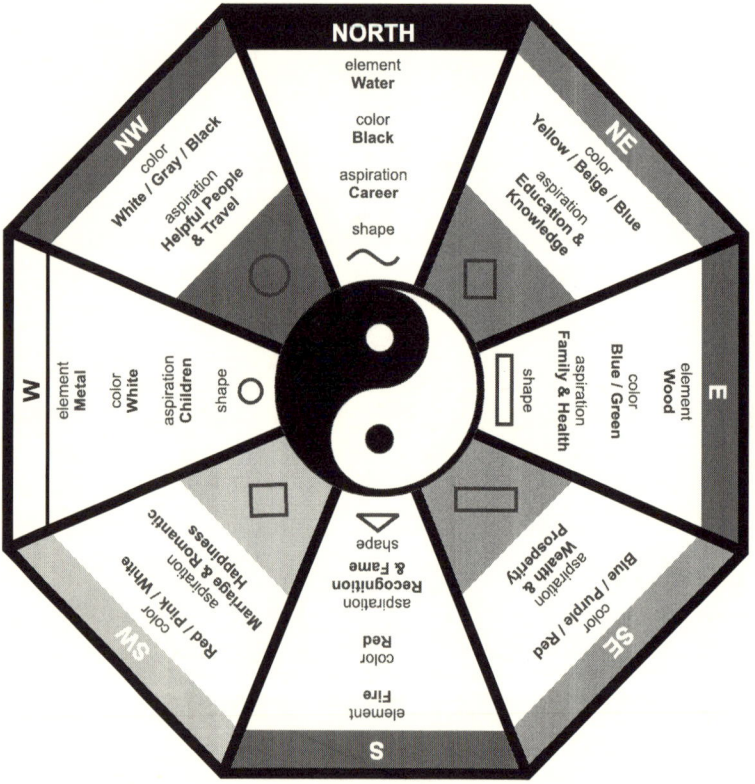

NORTH

element
Water

color
Black

aspiration
Career

shape

NE

color
Yellow / Beige / Blue

aspiration
**Education &
Knowledge**

NW

color
White / Gray / Black

aspiration
**Helpful People
& Travel**

W

element
Metal

color
White

aspiration
Children

shape

E

element
Wood

color
Blue / Green

aspiration
Family & Health

shape

SE

color
Blue / Purple / Red

aspiration
**Wealth &
Prosperity**

S

element
Fire

color
Red

aspiration
**Recognition
& Fame**

shape

SW

color
Red / Pink / White

aspiration
**Marriage & Romantic
Happiness**

WELCOME
HOME

CREATING WHAT YOU WANT
BY HOW YOU LIVE

By Sybilla Lenz
With Deborah Courville

BALBOA.
PRESS

A DIVISION OF HAY HOUSE

Balboa Press books may be ordered through booksellers or by contacting:

Balboa Press
A Division of Hay House
1663 Liberty Drive
Bloomington, IN 47403
www.balboapress.com
1-(877) 407-4847

Because of the dynamic nature of the Internet, any web addresses or links contained in this book may have changed since publication and may no longer be valid. The views expressed in this work are solely those of the author and do not necessarily reflect the views of the publisher, and the publisher hereby disclaims any responsibility for them.

The author of this book does not dispense medical advice or prescribe the use of any technique as a form of treatment for physical, emotional, or medical problems without the advice of a physician, either directly or indirectly. The intent of the author is only to offer information of a general nature to help you in your quest for emotional and spiritual well-being. In the event you use any of the information in this book for yourself, which is your constitutional right, the author and the publisher assume no responsibility for your actions.

Certain stock imagery © Thinkstock.
Any people depicted in stock imagery provided by Thinkstock are models, and such images are being used for illustrative purposes only.

ISBN: 978-1-4525-5342-9 (e)
ISBN: 978-1-4525-5343-6 (sc)
ISBN: 978-1-4525-5344-3 (hc)

Library of Congress Control Number: 2012910320

Printed in the United States of America

Balboa Press rev. date: 6/28/2012

DEDICATION

I am dedicating this book to all my wonderful friends through the years who helped shape who I was and who I have become. Each and every one of them gave me encouragement to go forward with my goals and dreams by being examples of unconditional love, humor, wisdom and possibility, to name a few. From Christine to Robin, Matt, Susan, Laura, Judy and Donna, they each showed me an aspect of myself that I could be. Last but not least my husband Jim who supports me in all I endeavor.

This book is also dedicated to all the seen and unseen energy that has helped me feel comforted in every home I have had since I was a child. I am grateful for the information on Feng Shui and Design that has enabled me to help others as well as myself create a better home, and to live in a place that I love, and that welcomes me every time I enter.

--SRL

"If nothing changes...nothing changes."

"As above, so below."

"The fact is, a person is so far formed by his surroundings, that his state of harmony depends entirely on his harmony with his surroundings"

TABLE OF CONTENTS

PREFACE

The meaning of home is "a place where a person or animal can find refuge and safety and live in security." OM is an ancient sacred syllable that is chanted in prayer and is symbolic of creation, destruction, and preservation. In my mind I feel they are one and the same thing.

When I speak with people about their homes, whether present or past, they all have feelings associated with them. Those feelings are either good or not so good, but they are present with those people every day.

Understanding the connection to our homes is essential to help us have more energy, connectivity, and peace in our lives. That peace and connectivity can be achieved whether home is a one room apartment or a 5200 square foot property, and can assist us in our aspirations to live healthy, wealthy, and peaceful lives.

A life we truly love is possible and supported by a home that is an intended space for all aspirations we seek in life. When a home is balanced energetically with the elements in our environment such as fire, earth, metal, water, and wood, it radiates a message of content. If a home is not balanced, it may broadcast discontent.

I was lucky enough to have worked with my co-author Deborah Courville in the practice of Feng Shui, and she experienced Feng Shui first hand. It is that which brought us together. Additionally, as a writer and a journalist, she has the skills to help create this book: one that shows that this art, while simple, can bring profound results.

'Welcome HOMe' is a collection of readable and engaging stories of the way various applications of Feng Shui helped change the energy of people's homes, and ultimately the energy of the occupants themselves. Feng Shui studies the physical science of energy, or Chi. Energy is present in everything; understanding how that energy affects us in our personal environments is helpful in bringing about positive change. Understanding and using that energy in the most effective way will also help make a home that is a welcoming and pleasant sanctuary.

ACKNOWLEDGEMENTS

Thanks to the folks at Keeler Printing for their help with the book cover image!

INTRODUCTION

Books about Feng Shui abound. Some are slender; others are thick. Some read like esoteric manuals on Eastern Mysticism. Others seem too basic to really mean much of anything.

Into this glut, if you will, of information about a very ancient Oriental practice, comes our book, 'Welcome HOMe.' In it, we give real life examples of how small Feng Shui inspired changes within people's homes have changed lives; we also try to make Feng Shui approachable, understandable--'welcoming' in fact. And that explains the first part of the title, 'Welcome.'

The reader will notice that in the second word of the title, 'Home,' the 'om' part of the word is either italicized or, as on the cover of the book, replaced by the Hindi Devanagari symbol for that syllable.

'Om' is pronounced as it looks with a long 'o' or sometimes as 'aum,' and has been used for millennia as an aid to meditation. Anyone living through, reading about, or listening to music of the 60's has probably encountered 'om.'

The idea for highlighting the fact that this ancient syllable is part of the English word 'home' was an inspiration that we then played with, inserting the Hindi symbol where feasible.

But the idea of ones home also being a peacefully energizing place of renewal and harmony--the object of meditation--is central to the concept of this book.

Feng Shui teaches that there are specific, naturally occurring paths that the earth's energy, or Chi, takes. Feng Shui suggests that allowing the energy to flow freely in ones home and enhancing the various elements that are natural to different portions of the home can help people achieve not only peaceful, harmonious dwellings but also places that energize and renew them. This, in turn, helps people realize their goals.

The stories in this book are all true. The principles of Feng Shui are used almost instinctively in the East and are incorporated so thoroughly into the fabric of daily life people there don't even really think about it. But you will notice, as you read, that many of the subjects in the stories contained in this book were drawn to certain areas of their living spaces for particular activities. Or they felt that something needed to be changed, but were not quite sure how.

This is 'natural knowing,' and it's something we all have, but are only in touch with to differing degrees.

Feng Shui allows us to bring ourselves more in touch with our 'natural knowing' and gives specific suggestions, remedies and steps to take that can bring about a home that will be both a refuge and a renewal, a place of tranquil harmony as well as a place of inspiration.

A place where, when one enters, one will truly feel: "Welcomed HOMe."

....

Classical Feng Shui

History & Symbolism

'FENG SHUI' MEANS 'WIND WATER' and speaks to the fact that the practice of Feng Shui seeks to align and balance people and their buildings with the forces of heaven (wind) and earth (water). Feng Shui is probably more than 5000 years old, but archaeologists have discovered written texts about the discipline from about 600 C.E. during the Tang Dynasty. Builders and carpenters in particular used pamphlets that listed directions and ways to measure and interpret earth formations: this was a very early use of Feng Shui.

In the 1960's during China's Cultural Revolution, the practice of Feng Shui was suppressed. However, since then, it has found a resurgence not only in the East but especially in the West.

Feng Shui grew out of the very ancient Oriental peoples' observation of the skies above them. Like other prehistoric societies, the Ancient Chinese were very much at the mercy of the seasons and the weather, and so sought to codify and perpetuate their observations. Think of Stonehenge in England, or the Great Pyramids in Egypt, or the Incan Pyramid of the Sun, or the Easter Island Monoliths: they all in some way are related to astronomical and seasonal events, such as solstices. In this way, early societies sought to relate themselves to the larger world, and to their place in the cosmos.

The use of the stars, and in particular the North or Pole Star which relative to the rest of the heavenly objects moves very little, makes sense when we realize that the magnetic compass was not invented until the eighth century in Europe. It was likely brought there by traders who went to the Orient, where lodestones had been used to determine the north-south axis for centuries. Just like early navigators who used Sextants and Astrolabes and other tools dependent on the movement and position of celestial bodies, the Ancient Chinese developed their own astronomical hypotheses and practices before they invented the compass, and had their own names for constellations such as the Big Dipper and Orion.

Feng Shui, like ancient Western philosophy and other mystic traditions, established certain 'elements.' Western thought is most familiar with four: earth, air, water and fire, whereas in the Orient and in Feng Shui we have five: metal, earth, fire, water and wood.

Combined with the movements of the stars, planets and our own Sun, these elements and their characteristics influence the physical world in which we live. Feng Shui seeks to take advantage of propitious influences and negate inauspicious ones as much as possible by understanding the elements and the celestial transitions.

The Chinese developed their compass or Luopan, which first used iron oxide (the 'lodestone') to indicate the north-south axis, in the second century C.E. The Luopan, however, differs from the Western compass in several ways. First, a Luopan points to the south magnetic pole; Western compasses point north. Another obvious difference is the intricate Feng Shui formulae on the cover of the Luopan. This is called the Heaven Dial; it sits on the Earth Plate, and rotates freely.

The Luopan has 24 directions, however, not just the usual four or eight on a Western compass. A Luopan allows 15 degrees for each direction; the entire circle, therefore, consists of 360 degrees, just like a Western compass. Interestingly enough, the Sun takes 15.2 days to go through a direction on a Luopan, so each degree on a Luopan equals roughly one day, and an entire circle of the Luopan equals a terrestrial year. Therefore, while the Luopan does measure earthly north–south, it also corresponds to the movement of the Earth around the Sun. This is another example of the way in which Feng Shui combines both earthly and celestial features.

In Classical Feng Shui, there are three major tools or theories practitioners use. First is the concept of Chi, or energy, called in various traditions prana, élan vital, or life force. Chi moves and shifts and fluctuates, it is not always static. This is why in Feng Shui it is important to allow the Chi to move freely, and also to take advantage of areas where the Chi most naturally flows.

The second theory is the concept of yin/yang or polarity. Yin/Yang, also called masculine/feminine, dry/wet, hot/cold is all about balance. The ideal state is a balanced state. Anyone who has ever had dizzy spells because of a fall, or due to substances such as alcohol or some medications will understand how disorienting it is--far from ideal! Feng Shui uses the concept of polarity and yin/yang to balance and align one's dwelling or other space so that all areas are harmonious, and the Chi flows freely through all the elements.

A companion concept to polarity is the theory of the five elements: metal, earth, fire, water and wood. This is called 'wu xing.' In Feng Shui, while these actual substances are used in various areas, it is their force, which is necessary to and inherent in life, which is most important.

The third theory or tool is the Bagua, or the energy template. This is based on the Luopan directions and incorporates the elements. It is used as a template and placed over the footprint of the home or building to which Feng Shui principles are being applied.

Classical Feng Shui developed into two major schools: Form and Compass, known as Ti Li and Li Chi. As we have seen above, Feng Shui grew out of ancient Chinese Astronomical study and the analysis of terrestrial features such as mountains, valleys, and bodies of water. As such, it makes sense that the Form or Landscape School of Feng Shui rose up first.

This Form School centers on the importance of choosing a site for building where the Chi is not stagnant or impeded. This school also developed the theory of the celestial animals: red phoenix, green dragon, white tiger, black turtle. It is not surprising that Chi is sometimes called 'Dragon Breath.' Finally, the concepts of yin/yang and the five elements were used to further refine the environment.

The use of animals and animal energies is another common practice among ancient peoples all over the globe; Native Americans are perhaps the best known New World practitioners of animal energy disciplines.

The Compass School of Feng Shui centers on the use of the Luopan or Chinese Compass, and emphasizes the four directions of North, South, East and West. There are many methods within this school including the Dragon Gate Eight Formation and Eight Mansions Methods.

Most Feng Shui practitioners do not adhere strictly to one school or the other, but use a blend of both. They may also incorporate elements from other traditions, particularly more modern schools of Feng Shui. You will most often find, therefore, as you will see in the chapters of this book, that Feng Shui consultants and Masters will use a Luopan, and a Bagua, and a combination of animal, color and element energies.

One fascinating feature of Feng Shui is the symbolic aspect, or the use of items with particular, iconic meaning to enhance various areas of the Bagua. Throughout this book we have talked about colors to use in various guas, and paintings, statues and other design features that are best situated in particular areas. Feng Shui has its own cadre of symbols, but it is most important that the client employ objects that they love, and that speak to them. If someone thinks an 'authentic Feng Shui symbol' is ugly, but uses it anyway, it probably won't work very well for them. The symbolic statues, flowers, paintings and so on speak to one's subconscious and it is vital that the person like, or even love, the object for its influence to make any difference.

Specific symbols bring specific energy and they are very powerful: that is why advertising companies pay millions of dollars to discover which picture, color, or shape will produce the effect they desire from their advertising.

In Feng Shui, a group of specialized items, animals, colors, flowers and so forth has developed to enhance specific aspirations. Since each area of the Bagua corresponds to different parts of a person's existence and aspirations, these Feng Shui symbols are best used in the area where enhancement is desired. Because

Feng Shui is an Oriental discipline, most of these symbols are uniquely Oriental. However, Western versions of them are also appropriate, and are just as effective, although some clients enjoy the particular Oriental flavor these items bring to their living and work spaces.

It might be good to point out here that in Asia, the art of flower arranging really is an art: people go to school for years to learn how to do it. And in addition to being pleasing to the eye and to the nose, the specific flowers in bouquets mean particular things. These symbolic meanings add to the subconscious message delivered by the arrangement. A related though much less disciplined practice became popular in the Renaissance, and again in Victorian times, and some gardeners and landscapers use the 'language of flowers' to convey specific messages in their creations.

For career, Feng Shui suggests using paintings, statues or figurines of horses and oxen, which signify success. Feng Shui also points to the narcissus as a symbol of the unveiling of hidden talents.

For wisdom and personal growth, symbols of the Buddha and lotus flowers are ideal.

For health, Feng Shui suggests butterflies, bamboo plants, cranes, and peacocks.

For wealth, Feng Shui suggests koi in an aquarium or pond, or a statue of a koi. Also, Chinese coins, an ox, a gem tree and peonies all symbolize prosperity. The money cat with paw upraised to welcome the flow of abundant Chi is also popular.

For fame or success, Feng Shui employs the chrysanthemum, as well as figurines or artwork depicting frogs and horses, which specifically are said to encourage a good reputation.

For relationship energy, Feng Shui suggests the use of dragon and phoenix together to symbolize unity and balance. Also, mandarin ducks signify pleasant relationships, as do hydrangeas. Here is is important to have pairs of things to boost the 'couple' energy.

For fertility or creativity, Feng Shui uses peaches, apples and other round fruits. Also orchids, which can additionally mean longevity or persistence depending on the aspiration.

For helpful spirits and protection, Feng Shui employs Fu dogs that you may see 'guarding' the entrance to a home. The chrysanthemum is related to good luck and protection. The elephant also signifies prudence and wisdom.

Once Feng Shui became popular in the West, modern Feng Shui Masters developed schools particularly for use by Western practitioners. The BTB or Black Hat Feng Shui is one of the most famous, and this school will be discussed in detail in the following chapter.

Classical and modern or contemporary Feng Shui differ mostly in how they use the Bagua, although there are of course other variations. Contemporary Feng Shui is more likely to incorporate ideas from modern science, psychology and other disciplines than is Classical Feng Shui. And while Classical Feng Shui determines the placement of the Bagua using compass directions and the Luopan, modern Feng Shui in particular BTB Feng Shui always situates the Bagua so the front door of the structure is in the north.

....

Black Sect Tantric Buddhist Feng Shui (BTB)

History & Symbolism

BTB, OR BLACK SECT TANTRIC BUDDHIST FENG SHUI, has evolved from centuries of use in Tibet, China and even India, and was brought to the Western world by Professor Lin Yun. His teachings have been studied and used here since the early 1970's, with many variations developing of his original work.

BTB has roots in the Bon religion, which pre-dates the conversion of the majority of Tibet to Buddhism. In the ninth and tenth centuries when this conversion occurred, many elements of the older Bon religion were incorporated into the Buddhism practiced in Tibet; now Bon is considered a branch of Tibetan Buddhism. This particular branch is called 'Black Sect,' and that is where the name Black Sect Tantric Buddhist Feng Shui comes from.

BTB embraces the old religion of Bon, yin/yang theory and the five element theory that covers the physical and metaphysical aspects of Feng Shui; this is similar to the way in which Native American shamans work with both physical and spiritual energies. In India, Vastu Shastra has been used for more than a millennium in the construction of buildings and homes and is quite similar to Classical and BTB Feng Shui with regard to the yin/yang theory and the five element theory.

All of these disciplines seek to encourage the best flow of Chi for the occupants of homes and buildings, and create environments that are beneficial.

There are three basic tenets in BTB Feng Shui and they echo those of Classical Feng Shui. But first it should be understood that BTB is not a religion, and it is not magic. BTB follows the principles of science and physics and incorporates these into Classical Feng Shui practices.

The first tenet is understanding the presence of Chi, or life force energy, which is present in all things. It is in the air we breathe, the homes we live in, the businesses we work in. It is in the animals and plants and all living things around us, both seen and unseen. Chi can be manipulated to move more slowly or more quickly, just as water in a stream can be dammed up, allowed to flow rapidly or diverted by gravel bars to create a meandering stream.

Unlike Classical Feng Shui, which uses a Luopan or Feng Shui compass, and also employs very intricate calculations, BTB uses a Bagua and studies physical shapes, colors and movement. Along with these analyses, BTB adjusts and manipulates Chi by using various enhancements or 'cures.'

The second tenet in BTB is to understand the way in which the yin /yang theory is present in our lives. Yin means the feminine aspect and is generally speaking light, flowing, soft, gentle, pale in color, soft in tone or voice. Yang means male and is generally speaking heavy, strong, darker in color, louder in tone. Some Feng Shui masters say there are seven dimensions of energy and the physical dimension is the one we are most accustomed to seeing. Therefore it is the one we most consider as a candidate for change. The yin/yang concept is crucial to examining and interpreting the environment correctly.

The physical dimension is more yang because three dimensional existence is dense; however, an object can become less yang and more yin if its color or weight changes, or even if it is moved.

BTB Feng Shui establishes multiple causes on many dimensions that are responsible to what a client or subject is experiencing. Thus, BTB Feng Shui is not only environmental, but spiritual and emotional as well. Many 'cures' are suggested for physical change, but many are also suggested for spiritual or causal change since BTB practitioners believe that a person's experience can be changed by using both physical and metaphysical cures.

In Classical Feng Shui, practitioners use visible, tangible factors to effect change. They use the Luopan, and utilize birth data to determine the change or alteration needed to produce the outcome desired. In BTB Feng Shui, practitioners use both physical and metaphysical approaches to effect change, but lean more heavily to the metaphysical.

When the Chi is adjusted so it is more abundant and balanced with yin/yang theory it can energize us in ways that allow us to be healthier and more productive. Other examples of yin/yang are: sweet/sour, passive/aggressive, cold/hot, down/up, light/dark, back/front, below/above, soft/firm. Some questions to ask yourself about your environment to analyze the yin/yang balance might be: is the lighting too dim or bright? Is the color of the room pretty and soft or heavy and dark? Are the sounds you hear pleasant? Do you feel heavy or light and uplifted? The Chi of an individual can be changed by changing the yin/yang balance of the environment's energy. Good Chi can aid life aspirations and enhance and attract loving relationships. It can improve good fortune and create better health, encouraging deeper sleep. Sleep deprivation is rampant in our culture, and causes many health issues.

The third tenet in BTB Feng Shui is understanding the five element theory. Again, the five elements are found in both Classical Feng Shui and BTB Feng Shui.

The five elements are fire, earth, metal, water and wood; they are found all around us, both inside and outside.

Wood energy is expansive and growing energy. Think of how wood relates to springtime, sunrise in the east, and the colors of green, blue and brown. This energy also resonates in rectangles, and of course in living plants and flowers. Its position is the east and southeast areas of the Bagua and Luopan.

Fire energy is that of the sun; it moves rapidly, like a fire. It is represented by the color red and resonates with pyramidal or triangular shapes. It is found in the south area of the Bagua and Luopan.

Earth energy is solid and grounding: rocks, earth, brick, and adobe. It resonates with square shapes and is found in the northeast, southwest and center of the Bagua and Luopan. The colors of earth are represented by yellow, beige and all earthen tones typical of late summer and autumn.

Metal energy is energy that is waning or closing down. It is found in the west area of the Bagua and Luopan. The colors of gold, silver and white resonate with metal energy as do circular and cylindrical shapes. This energy is helpful to slow or contract Chi.

Water energy can be flowing or still, as needed. It is found in the north area of the Bagua and Luopan It is represented by waving or undulating shapes, and the colors are shades of blue, and black.

Understanding the Chi, the yin/yang theory and the five element theory in our environment is very important in BTB because our environments dictate what we feel and think and what actions we take--or do not take.

As you might guess once you read the stories in this book, and now you know the backgrounds of Classical and BTB Feng Shui, which are both used to best advantage in this book's examples, the concept of Chi, of yin/yang, and of the five elements in Feng Shui are extremely impactful to both our environments and ourselves.

A quick example might be if you were to inherit your Great Aunt Martha's house. You remember this house from 25 years ago when you were a child. As you arrive, you go up the front steps and realize they haven't been repaired or painted in the last two decades. The front door has chipped paint and the door knocker is hanging sideways.

When you go inside, you smell the old attic smell of the house and the furnishings. You see the steps in front of you leading to the second floor, and they are loaded with items stored on each stair tread all the way up and down.

On the second floor you come to the largest bedroom, which you enter. The room is dark and the curtains are old and heavy. The bed is covered in a dark velvet spread and has a low hanging canopy over it. The room smells old, stale, and the fireplace in the room is dank and unused. The paint is dark and smoke stained.

Notice how you feel about this room. Would you want to spend the night here without first cleaning and de-cluttering this home?

When you entered the house, consider the fact that your personal Chi changed because it was affected by the Chi of the house, the unbalanced yin/yang and the improper placement of the five elements.

This is just an example, but we are all affected by our homes, and by everything around us, everywhere we go, by Chi, yin/yang, and the five elements that are the critical tenets of BTB Feng Shui.

The last point to discuss about BTB Feng Shui is the metaphysical dimensions and how we can effect transcendental cures in this area. For thousands of years, the Feng Shui masters of the Orient and the Indian sub continent, and more recently of the West, have applied prayers, meditations and physical; chants and mudras (symbolic gestures) to affect the energy in their environment. The goal is to improve their own selves, and manifest their highest aspirations.

Using prayers or mantras is helpful in transcendental cures because prayers and mantras have a higher vibration than the physical written request. In The Intention Experiment, Lynne McTaggart says that our prayers and intentions do affect the energy of ourselves and others, and can also be physically measured.

The next level of cures includes, but is not limited to, intention cures using red envelopes in certain areas of the Bagua. A person can also use light cures, water cures, crystal cures, color cures, sound cures, and more to manipulate the energy of an area, as you will see in the stories in this book. Once the Chi has been adjusted, and the yin/yang balanced, and the five elements brought into alignment, then the Chi of the person in the space has also been changed.

Using mudras are a great yin reinforcement to the physical or yang cure used because this mudra uses metaphysical energy to

raise mind, body and speech to a higher vih
an extremely powerful technique and m?
Feng Shui masters to help a client add an
energy to the area requiring adjustment.

An example of a mudra technique follows. It shoun.
used once an area has been thoroughly cleaned, cleared, ana ~
space clearing done. This is called a three secrets reinforcement
cure.

Meridians flow through our fingers and toes; meridians are
the paths energy most easily takes. Stand in the area you wish to
reinforce and hold your hands together with the thumbs facing up
and the fingers intertwined, except for the first two fingers. Point
these two fingers of both hands, with the two thumbs up, in the
direction of the Bagua you are working in. Now, visualize your
desire being fulfilled and at the same time say a mantra such as 'om
mani padme om.' Repeat the mantra nine times. This reinforces
the area and completes the physical and metaphysical components
for enhancing change.

There are many other mudras or symbolic gestures, and a
multitude of other mantras you may find more comfortable to
use, or more to your liking.

·························

Career & Life Purpose

North/Water

WHEN YOU READ ABOUT AND EMPLOY FENG SHUI PRINCIPLES or practice Feng Shui cures and strategies, you will notice a lot of emphasis on the entryway, better known as the door or mouth of Chi, or energy.

The different schools of Feng Shui emphasize the front of a home or building in a few different ways. In classical Feng Shui, the front door is where the largest amount of Chi will enter the home or business. Classical Feng Shui uses specific and precise calculations based on actual compass directions and periods of time. BTB Feng Shui, or 'Black Sect Tantric' Feng Shui, brought to Western culture by Professor Lin, uses a template called a Bagua. The Bagua is placed over the floor plan of the home or business with the front door always positioned in the north, even though that may not be true north on a compass.

Some people use entrances to their homes that are not the front doors to their homes, such as a side door or garage door. The Bagua template is still placed over the front entrance to the home or building, after thorough analysis of the perimeter has been done.

BTB Feng Shui philosophy teaches that everything is energy, called Chi, and that the mouth of Chi is positioned at the actual front door of the home or building. This position is always considered to be north.

To complete the Bagua, if north is where one enters, moving to the left we have northeast, then east, then southeast, south, southwest, west, northwest and back to north. You may refer to the Bagua map on the Frontispiece of this book to see this more clearly.

This method can be confusing when determining how to place the Bagua or whether or not to use BTB or classical Feng Shui. What follows is a story illustrating that very confusion surrounding the front door.

Samantha's Story:

The year was 1999 and Samantha was having her first consultation for Feng Shui. Samantha had a list of things she wanted to work on: career, relationships, children, and moving her residence. She had just finished reading a book on Feng Shui that spoke about how we limit our lives, and what Feng Shui can help us with. She thought, 'if this does work, then I am going for it all!'

Her home had a ground floor entrance to a home office that covered the entire ground floor. The upstairs entrance opened to the residence, which included a living room, dining room, kitchen, three bedrooms and a bathroom.

When the consultant arrived at Samantha's home, she entered through the downstairs office entrance. There was an outside stairway to the right of the downstairs entrance; this led up to the door to the upstairs entrance. This door did not face the same direction as did the ground floor door.

What do you do with this situation in Feng Shui? The consultant was schooled in BTB Feng Shui and so placed the Bagua over the bottom entrance and the top entrance the same way, positioning north at both entrance doors. However, the bottom door faced people walking up to it while the top door faced directly right, or east.

This seemed confusing to Samantha.

The consultant began at the basement door; according to BTB Feng Shui this north entrance is the career entrance. Samantha was congratulated because the path to the bottom entrance was clear and uncluttered, and the door swung open easily. In all schools of Feng Shui it is very important to have doors swing open freely, with no obstructions.

Once inside the office, the consultant said there was entirely too much clutter. Things needed to be neat and orderly. On one side of the basement was a single car garage with the usual amount of things that were not properly stored. Once again, the message was: this needs to be cleaned and straightened, de-cluttered.

Feng Shui teaches that the reason clutter and disorganization is so important is because when Chi enters our homes and buildings, it needs to be able to flow and circulate easily and effortlessly. This ensures that we are always being nurtured by fresh and flowing Chi instead of stagnant Chi--like the dead air in an old closet that hasn't been used or cleaned out for years.

Feng Shui also teaches that we should always consider doing a thorough 'space clearing' of existing areas we occupy as well as newly acquired properties. When cleaning and decluttering any area of the Bagua, it is important to clear that space not only physically but energetically; there are many techniques that are suggested for this including burning incense, burning candles, hand clapping, and bell ringing.

The next question Samantha asked the consultant was how to bring her business upstairs to what was now her residence, and prepare to move her home out to a quiet woodland property where she had always wanted to live. The consultant suggested she begin to bring her office books and files upstairs and slowly turn the upper floor from a residence to an office. The consultant also suggested that Samantha change the chair she usually sat in at the dining room table to a different one, one where she could see the changes she was making in the space. In this way, her body would begin to incorporate and internalize the changes and begin to function from the new perspective.

With her work cut out for her, Samantha took the suggestions seriously and went to work. She de-cluttered and straightened, organizing every square inch of the ground level. She put all her files into proper order. It was tough, at first, but she found eventually that it was easier to work from organized files. The indoor stairway leading up to the residence from the office was lined with things that needed to go up or downstairs. Samantha took everything off the steps and put it all away where it belonged. This encouraged a free flow of energy up and down the stairs and between floors.

Samantha quite enjoyed the change: the step clutter had been a source of annoyance to her. What a difference it made to have those stairs open and clear. After seeing what a difference cleaning and de-cluttering had made, Samantha took the final step and did a thorough space clearing on the entire property. She used a sage incense and wafted the smoke through each room of the property, paying special attention to the closets, corners and basement areas where Chi can become stagnant.

Samantha also discovered a real sense of inner excitement after the initial consultation, and the excitement continued whenever she would think about Feng Shui or what else she needed to do. She also found her *office felt much better being organized. Her mind could now focus on what was in front of her instead of being distracted by the mess. Samantha felt, and therefore became, more productive. Her career started to really take off, and one filing cabinet of client files soon became three. Within two years, Samantha's office had been completely moved to the upper level of the building, and she had moved her home out, to her new residence in the woods.*

Feng Shui is such a wonderful tool to utilize in dreams and ambitions because not only does it help you create that which you intend, it gives you a great feeling of joy and accomplishment because you 'feel good.'

Another great example of Feng Shui and how important it is with regard to the front door comes from Laura.

Laura's Story:

Laura asked for a consultation in Feng Shui because she had a home based business and felt something was stopping her from really expanding, despite some attempts with advertising and other tactics. She had heard that Feng Shui can sometimes be helpful.

At that time, I had been studying Feng Shui formally for more than five years and had begun to see amazing and positive changes in people's lives who used it. So I told Laura I would take a look and offer her some suggestions.

The first thing I noticed when I drove into her property was that the driveway led to two huge garage doors, but the entrance to the house was far to the right. This made me feel uncertain about how I should actually enter the house.

This is significant, because the entrance to the home should be easily distinguishable, not only for visitors but for the Chi as well.

When I did find the front door, I discovered that it was an old door, painted white, with chipped paint in a few spots. The hardware on the door was tarnished. The steps leading up to the door also seemed to be wobbly, and the mat in front of the door was small and worn.

Once inside Laura's home, I found it welcoming, orderly and aesthetically appealing. However, upon entering her office, my first thought was, 'oh my gosh, this has so much stuff!' There were open shelves with books and papers and her desk was oddly positioned in the room.

Laura told me that day she did not feel comfortable working at her desk in its present position, so that was one of the first things we needed to correct.

But before we began that, I told Laura that her office needed to be made orderly. Clutter needed to disappear and the shelves needed to have covers or doors so that the books, files and paperwork were tidied away and not visible.

I checked Laura's date of birth and established the best working and sleeping direction for her body and mind. It turned out her desk was not placed facing one of her best and most useful directions, so I suggested she move the desk so it did face one of her best directions. Laura also took my suggestion about covering the open shelves so that the materials of her business, when not in specific use, were not visible. This gave the office a much more calm and focused, and a more professional atmosphere.

Then we turned to the rest of the house. The front door faced east. I explained to Laura that she could lay the Bagua over her home's floor plan in BTB fashion, or work with the natural compass directions of classical Feng Shui. She chose to use the classical method to orient the front door. Since her door faced east according to classical Feng Shui, I suggested she change the color of the door. I also suggested she invest in new hardware and fix the steps to create a more solid approach to the door.

Laura chose to have the front entrance steps completely rebuilt. She also replaced the front door with a new one, and a beautiful new storm door. The changes were amazing. The front steps now curved around and faced anyone driving into the property. This brought attention to the front door from the vantage point of the driveway, a crucial and positive change as it was now unmistakable where the entrance of the home was. As visitors walked up the curving steps to the lovely front door, they not only felt invited in, they were eager to go inside.

Laura's career is flourishing, and she says that she attributes a big part of her career success to the changes Feng Shui encouraged her to make to the front entrance of her home business, and to her office.

....

Wisdom & Self Actualization

Northeast/Earth

WHEN I THINK ABOUT THE NORTHEAST SECTION OF THE GUA, or area of my home, I wonder about all the places I have lived so far. I wonder if any of them was significant in my constant drive and desire to know the wisdom of the universal teachings and to create a life I could love. I never felt content or fully happy with my life or myself for countless reasons, and I was always searching for more information that might lead me to the wonderful place of truly being happy with my life. I certainly had read and listened to enough people who professed that it was entirely possible to have a life you love, with all your needs met.

I now believe this is true. I now can say I really do live a life that I love, and I have so much gratitude for the wisdom and information that has come to me from so many sources for all these years. Looking back, I always had a place in every home where there was a collection of books, tapes, articles, or pictures of things that aided me, or represented the life I was looking for. In every house of mine, there was a table or a stand, or an entire wall of information on higher wisdom. Some people have entire rooms in their homes devoted to a sacred space for meditation, inner insight, or personal rest and rejuvenation.

Consider the following suggestions for creating your personal sanctuary inside your home.

The word 'OM,' pronounced 'AUM') is the sacred syllable of Hinduism, and represents God, or Brahma, the source of all existence. OM represents the three qualities inherent in the cosmic vibration:

A - represents Brahma, creation

U - represents Vishnu, preservation

M - represents Shiva, transmutation

It is possible to transform your home into a place that exudes a peaceful and secure resonance similar to the highest cosmic vibration. In some cultures, it is taught that when you feel this vibration within you, you will transform your physical reality and experience to reflect that, creating a peaceful, beautiful and abundant life.

The space governing wisdom and self actualization is in the northeast area or gua of your home. You may refer to the Bagua map on the Frontispiece of this book to see this more clearly.

Do a thorough cleaning and de-cluttering of the area, including moving out furniture and taking pictures off the walls, and even taking window treatments down. Now that you have physically cleared and cleaned the area, the energy of the space needs to be space cleared. You may use any one of many techniques to clear the energy of the space from any thing that might linger there from prior owners, or from other people who spent time there.

A popular technique is to light a white candle and think with intention about clearing and releasing. You could also move through the area methodically burning incense: white sage is particularly recommended. Let the smoke permeate the area. You could also clap your hands from floor to ceiling, or ring a bell.

Upon completing your chosen clearing technique, sit in the space and mentally intend that this will now be your space for accessing higher wisdom. Accessing higher wisdom, or meditation, can be either formal or simple. Use what works for you. Even if you just make a practice of sitting in your space for a few minutes each day, thinking about your goals, asking for guidance, and mentally making a plan, you will be using your innate link to higher wisdom, and reap the benefits.

This northeast area of the gua is linked to the earth element. For color in your meditation space, therefore, you may wish to use earthy colors like yellow, beige or brown. You could enhance this area by using items from the earth such as stones and crystals. Even if this room or area of your home serves a specific function, for example, if it is a kitchen or a dining room, you can use the colors and elements suggested by Feng Shui and create a space that subtly speaks to your higher self. You may be surprised by the way in which you are drawn to sit, perhaps, at the dining room table, or stand at the kitchen sink gazing out the window, for a few minutes each day to meditate, pray or just quiet your mind and focus.

The following story represents one person's example of using a space in the northeast section of a home for daily meditation and healing intentions.

Ava's Story:

Ava's house was a beautiful little log home nestled in the woods. She called for a consultation to enhance the relationship area of her home. Being familiar with Feng Shui, she had also had first hand results using some of its techniques. When she purchased her home, she had already employed some Feng Shui principles in the set up and move, and in the way she decorated her home.

One of the things that was immediately obvious was that Ava meditated: she fully believed in the power to heal and self heal through visualization and various other techniques she had studied over the years.

As we walked through her home, she led me upstairs to an area that was a small bedroom in the northeast gua. This was her meditation area, and it was almost perfect. The room had many stones and crystals placed around it, and all Ava's books on healing and self care were stored here. There was a lovely chair and mat for her use in meditation and the room was painted a soft earthy yellow color.

The only issue in the room was a sloped ceiling, since the room was tucked up under one of the house's eaves. I suggested to Ava that if she hung a crystal from the ceiling in the center of the room it would offset the effect of the sloping ceiling. This would encourage movement of Chi and counteract the downward pressure the slanted could cause to anyone sitting under it.

To create this place of wisdom for yourself, you may wish to use this sample meditation.

Sit comfortably in a relaxed position with your spine straight and your legs and arms uncrossed. Start by noticing your breath moving through your body as you breathe in and out. After two or three cleansing breaths, close your eyes and take a long breath in, filling your entire body and at the same time seeing light along with the breath coming in and filling and cleansing your body from head to toe.

While you are doing this, move your head slowly down resting your chin on your chest, breathe in raising your head to the center and all the way back as far as it will comfortably go. As you exhale, slowly bring your head forward until your chin is resting on your chest again. Take another deep cleansing breath in, bringing your head up, centered, and back. Then release the breath slowly, and as you exhale blow the air through your teeth while you lower your head back to your chest.

Do this for seven or eight times and then when you have finished, bring your head back to its normal central position, and be still. Notice that your body feels light and airy, your mind's stream of thought seems to be calmer, and you feel quiet inside and out. If your mind still seems busy, do another set of inhalations and exhalations until it is still. Keep your eyes closed, and practice listening to your breath, and visualize light coming in as you breathe.

This is a simple but powerful exercise and promises to help you find that calm and peaceful place inside you. Once you have energized the space in the northeast gua with your intent for higher wisdom, and begun meditating daily, you will experience your life changing in amazing ways.

CHAPTER FIVE

· ·

Family & Community

East/Wood

YEARS AGO WHEN I HAD MY FIRST CONSULTATION, I remember asking how I could bring my family closer by using Feng Shui. My two boys were 13 years apart, and I wanted them to have a closer relationship.

Because east is the area of the home, or gua, governing families and community, it was suggested that I place pictures of my children on the east wall of my home. I was encouraged to use wooden frames, since wood is the element that resonates in the east. It was also suggested that I weave a symbolic green ribbon among the pictures, to tie them all together. The element of wood is linked to the colors of green and brown.

A couple of weeks after I did this, I noticed that the boys seemed to talk more with each other, and go places together quite agreeably. This was exactly the change I had wished for, and it was the springboard to an overall better relationship between my sons that progressed with the years.

The east area of the gua is to the left as you enter the front door of your home. The front door is always north, even if it actually doesn't face that way. You may refer to the Bagua map on the Frontispiece of this book to see this more clearly.

Along with the element wood and the colors of green or brown, rectangular shapes and live plants complement and enhance this gua.

Here is one woman's story of the way the energy of a loved one affected not only one room but the whole house, and of how she transformed that energy from sadness to fond remembrance.

Karine's Story:

That day I came home from work to find the door to Mom's bedroom closed, just as I'd left it that morning when I had left. I knew something was wrong. It was too quiet. I opened the door to the bedroom and found her. My heart sank with the heaviness of her loss. My Mom was gone.

Once the funeral home had come and taken her body, I shut the door to her room and just could not imagine going back in there. The house felt empty and I felt lost. I felt awful.

About two weeks passed, and I decided to go into Mom's room and begin putting her things away. It was really tough to do this, especially the little things, like taking Mom's tooth brush out of its holder.

Mom had always kept a stuffed bear on her bed and while I was in there putting her things away, I took the bear and put some of Mom's jewelry on it: her watch, a favorite pair of earrings, a pin, a string of pearls. Then I placed it back on the bed where she had kept it, and hoped the room wouldn't seem so empty now.

My daughter was 11, soon to be 12, and she missed her Nana terribly. I began to leave the door to Mom's room open a bit instead of shutting it. And then one evening I invited my daughter to come with me and read a story on her Nana's bed.

That first night was rough, and my daughter could not stay in the room. But we tried again the next night, and even though it was difficult, we did it. Having the stuffed bear dressed in Mom's jewelry helped: it made us feel like part of Mom was still with us.

My daughter and I continued to read on her Nana's bed every evening, and soon we started to giggle and enjoy spending time once again in Mom's room.

A few months later, I was sitting one evening trying to watch television. Each time I looked over at Mom's empty place on the couch I would feel her loss all over again. I mentioned this to my husband, and we cried together, but then decided maybe it was time to move the furniture in the room around a bit.

That weekend we did this, and the room immediately felt better. We were no longer looking at the empty place where Mom used to sit. The house still felt sad and empty to me, but it did feel a little bit better.

We all felt the heavy sadness, and we even considered selling our home. For six more months this feeling haunted us until I got a thought again: why not turn the bedroom that had been Mom's into an office?

Once my mind was made up, the process began. Boxing up all her things to give away was very difficult, since it seemed like I wanted to forget Mom, and that was completely opposite from how I felt.

Then I got another idea. Mom had always loved lighthouses, and had a collection of figurines, pictures and snow globes on that theme. Rather than remove Mom from the new office, I decided to decorate the space with the lighthouse theme. I incorporated Mom's lighthouse collection along with new decorative elements, and re-painted and re-decorated that room.

The entire nature and energy of the room had lifted from sadness and loss to light and hope. I began to feel that Mom would always be with us, shining in our hearts and memories just like a lighthouse beacon. The change was immediate: the room was no longer the place my Mom had passed away in, it was a comfortable work space that felt warm and inviting, and the change was very positive for everyone. The idea of her light continuing to shine on us through her lighthouses seemed perfect, too.

The following summer, the final touch came when I decided I wanted to have a garden stone in memory of my Mom. She loved the flowers in our garden, and once again this was a way to remember her every time we worked in the garden. My daughter and I went down to the river, and soon found the 'perfect' stone. The stone was very large and too heavy for us to lift, so we made a sling and dragged it back to the car. All the while, we asked Mom to help us accomplish our task.

We got the stone into the car, and took it to the engraver. It took two men to get it out of the car and they were in awe, not believing that my daughter and I had loaded the stone into the car by ourselves. We had it engraved with a beautiful rose, and the words: 'Mom - Forever in our Hearts.'

After getting the stone back from the engraver, my daughter and I couldn't get it out of the car. When my husband came home, he could barely lift it, but somehow he managed to get it out of the car and into the garden where we wanted it. He did it himself...or did he? Maybe my Mom helped all of us during the different parts of the journey to find that stone and bring it home. We believe that Mom was helping us and showing us that she approved of all the changes we had made.

Mom is and always will be in our hearts, and from the day I knew she was gone it has been a multitude of baby steps that we all took to move forward without her, and turn our house back into a home again.

This story illustrates one person's feelings of losing a loved family member, and the energy felt when her mother died, and how she was able to transform that energy. The other point this story illustrates is one often forgotten in practicing Feng Shui: the outside of the property.

Some Feng Shui masters say that the land is more important than the house, and the house is more important than the occupants. When you look at your home and property don't forget to extend the Bagua (energy template) over your home and outward over the land around your house. That way you can enhance the energy of the land along with your home in each area of the gua, paying special attention to those areas that you wish to improve, or intend to focus on.

In this situation, the healing of the family was extremely important to Karine and her family and one of the things she instinctively did was to create a living and beautiful garden in remembrance of her mother. Wood energy is represented by living plants, and can be manifested outside in the garden as well as inside the home with a lovely plant display in the east area of the home.

East relates to family and community, and also resonates with health. Here is a story illustrating that.

Sarah's Story:

I had recently had back surgery, and felt completely hopeless because I was practically bedridden with pain. The doctor told me that there was nothing more that could be done. That was a terrible message to hear and try to digest. I was in intense despair when my friend the Feng Shui master suggested a consultation.

She came to my home, and we talked about my back problem along with the past heartache of losing two of my three children. I told her about my husband's stroke, and how we both had been absorbed in trying to overcome severe health issues that plagued us at the same time we were dealing with the emotional blow of losing our sons.

The Feng Shui master suggested a general space clearing throughout our apartment and then focused on my bedroom, because that was where I was spending most of my time. On the dresser, which happened to be in the east corner of the house, she suggested that I create a space dedicated to health and healing. She suggested I bring in pictures of my family so I could see them every day, and place other things there that represented health to me.

I placed fruit in that space. I placed pictures of my boys and of my friends, and I did notice that I really loved being able to look at that every day. My Feng Shui master also suggested hanging some artwork on the east wall to represent wood energy: prints of a forest, or of springtime. She suggested a bubbling fountain could promote wood energy natural to the east. Once I did all of that, I just loved my little peaceful, happy spot.

Within a couple of months, my doctor contacted me and said he had consulted with another physician who had agreed, after reviewing my case, to operate again on my back to see if the pain could be relieved or at least lessened.

I was elated!

I had the second surgery and my back improved dramatically. Before long I was able to be up and around and felt more like my old self.

In this situation, a 'health altar' as it is called in Feng Shui, was created in the area of family or wood energy in the east. Creating such a space promoted health and well being. The combination of a thorough space clearing, particularly when someone has been ill, and the creation of a focal point that radiates positive feelings will result in significant and positive change.

....

Wealth & Prosperity

Southeast/Wood

IF YOU'RE LIKE MOST PEOPLE, you turned to this chapter on Wealth right away, or at least as one of the first chapters you wanted to check out!

We all want to be prosperous. We live in a society obsessed with wealth and prosperity. But the purpose of this chapter is not to bemoan or endorse that fact. Rather, the purpose of this chapter is to look at the various forms wealth may take in a person's life, and to share a specific story or two about how shifting the Chi and creating space for wealth and prosperity to enter a life has worked for real people.

Wealth, of course, means money: cash, property, investments or a mix of all three, wealth gives a person the power to buy. This in turn can give that person the power to do. We often see a direct result of this particular kind of wealth=power=action in political campaigns, where the candidate with the most money is also the one blanketing the airwaves and billboards. A more sanguine example might be people like Bill Gates who have made millions and who also give millions every year to charity. And that's an important thing to remember about prosperity: to have it, you must share it. Money, like everything else according to the teachings of Feng Shui, is energy. Therefore, it must circulate, and not stagnate.

Wealth is also associated, less familiarly however, with what a person has: health, intellect, talent, etc. These are all separate and other sections of the Bagua and also of this book, so they won't be discussed here.

The section of the Bagua that resonates with wealth is in the southeast. You may refer to the Bagua map on the Frontispiece of this book to see this more clearly.

However--and this is a big 'however'--as we discuss wealth here, please keep in the forefront of your mind not only the other types of 'wealth' besides money, but also the concept of wealth or prosperity as a means to an end.

In an effective life, wealth can be just that: the means to an end, not an end in and of itself. In Feng Shui, it is suggested that clients' goals not be to have money simply to have it, to be like that king from Sing a Song of Sixpence: 'sitting in his counting house counting all his money.'

Feng Shui teaches that we view wealth, i.e., having money, as a means to live a vibrant and effective life. Think of all the things you may say to yourself with regard to money, and then complete this sentence with no fewer than three objects: 'if I could afford it I would--'

What did you say?

Did you say, 'fix up my house' or 'quit my job' or 'buy a new car' or 'help other people' or 'travel' or something else?

Whatever you said, wealth, for you, is the conduit to shaping the material (and if you said 'help other people' spiritual to some degree) part of your world.

We are foolish if we try to say we aren't material. Unless you are a mystic ascetic, we all live in the material world.

But what we choose to do with our material wealth, and how we view it, are key to our living effective lives and not being mired in materialism, blind to the spiritual and emotional aspects of life.

Okay. So you want wealth. And you have your reasons, your 'to do list' of what prosperity will enable you to do.

How to start?

First, think about coming from abundance. That's a tricky thing to do if you're eating pasta four nights a week and wearing hand me downs. But it's all about shifting how you view things, and about taking small steps to start living the life you want.

Vicki's Story

I grew up in the 60's and so I'd heard about Eastern mysticism including Feng Shui. I bought a book on Feng Shui in the 90's and got very confused when I read it. I did try to do a few things, but it seemed like such a massive undertaking I stopped.

I realize now that this was because I was approaching Feng Shui not from a place of adjusting my physical (and also my internal) space to free up Chi and attract wealth. I was approaching it as an overlay, an addition, a further cluttering of my home.

When I approached it as a chance to make room for wealth and prosperity, things worked much better.

I wanted to create wealth and prosperity in my life; although I usually had 'enough' I didn't have 'enough for what I wanted,' and I always felt I was just a little bit short. I certainly didn't have enough money to be charitable with, and I also found myself growing very stingy, miserly and bitter, feelings I didn't like in either myself or in others.

It's all very well to say, 'money isn't everything,' and it isn't, but I find that it's mostly people who have money who say this, and also that having money makes dealing with almost everything else much easier. Even good health, which money can't buy, is assisted through good diet and proper medication, both of which money <u>can</u> buy.

I turned to Feng Shui to see if I was unknowingly keeping money out of my life, not attracting the prosperity I felt I deserved. And that was the first step: look at what I had and eliminate or change or clear it so that I could make space for something better to come in.

First, I found the wealth area of my living space. That's the south east corner of your home.

Then I cleaned it, touching up any paint or wallpaper that might have been peeling. I got rid of any decorations that were made up of dried plant material, twigs, etc. I burned a stick of incense to help lean the energy, too.

Next, I looked at the space critically and shifted or moved anything that didn't signal 'wealth' to me. For example, on the lower level of my house, the litter box was smack dab in the wealth section. I moved it a couple of feet over. The cat didn't even notice. Upstairs, I moved a painting I love but that didn't signal 'wealth' or 'prosperity' to me: it's an Albrecht Dürer portrait of Don Quixote. It's beautiful, but it doesn't belong in the prosperity area of a living space.

Then I looked at the color of the walls. In the prosperity section of a living space, walls are ideally a rich, warm color, maybe even gold, to suggest money. Mine was a deep apricot on one floor, and wood panelling on the lower floor, and I left them that way since they worked for me.

One big obstacle was that my bathroom was located right in my prosperity segment. If you have this structural challenge there are things you can do to offset this, just as I did. I began closing the bathroom door routinely; this was so the Chi wouldn't go right down the drains. I also hung a mirror on the door, to reflect the energy and keep it from being lost in the bathroom and down the drains. I chose a fairly large sunburst design mirror, but you could use any kind of mirror, even an inexpensive stick up one, or a 'found' one from a jumble sale that you use as is or transform with a can of gold spray paint.

Okay, now I'd cleared away negative influences, things that subconsciously spoke of 'dried, miserly, ruined,shrunken, old' etc. and laid the foundation for creating my wealth area. I was making space for good things.

I got a green frog shaped planter and put it in this area, and I put my change into it. Each week, I cleaned out my change purse and visualized that money building, and acting as a lure to draw more money to me.

If you say you can't afford to just put money in a jar or a planter and not use it, do what I did: only put change in your planter or your jar that you don't like. Start with pennies, but have faith and add more when you can. I, personally, don't like nickels and pennies much. So I put them in for the first year or so, and kept the quarters and dimes in my purse. Now I do clean my entire purse out.

And although using a decorative planter is nice, if you don't happen to have one laying around, a jar will do.

Next, I took a wander through my living space, on the lookout for things that spoke to me of prosperity, things I could put in my new 'prosperity corner.' I dug through drawers, cupboards, closets and book cases and found a number of things, some I'd even forgotten I had. (Sometimes long forgotten things buried in places like that hold no appeal and therefore are best recycled, but if you still love something you re-discover, that's perfect). I re-decorated the wealth section of my living space with some--not necessarily all--of these things. I focused on gold frames, jewels and coins, things of that nature. I had to be sure not to make it look cluttered or tatty, and remember that I was creating in this space what I wanted to attract and create in my larger life. I made sure things in this space were things I liked.

In the lower level of my house, I moved all of my personal files to that area (after I moved the litter box!) and when I look at them, I see all my holdings whether it's property, or bank accounts, or insurance policies, or photos from trips, or diplomae from educational institutions, etc. When I see this, I feel good.

In those same areas, I hung pictures of luxury locales, royalty, money, and anything else that said 'wealth' to me. I found myself moving pictures from all over my house as I did this and that's great: that's the whole idea, to move and change and free up the space so the Chi can move and the wealth can come in. I did this and it was also great exercise!

You might say, 'but I don't have the money to go buy pictures.' Okay fair enough. Again, use what you have and what you may dig out of places you have stashed things. You will probably re-discover things you'd forgotten you had! I did, and 'resurrecting' something you love and forgot you owned fosters that feeling of wealth. Stop at your local thrift store or yard sales. Tear out a picture from a magazine or print one off the internet.You can start small, and it's better to start with one or two things that you love, and that mean 'wealth and prosperity' to you than to clutter the space with items that don't particularly resonate. You can always add as things come to you. And the weird thing is, if you imagine what you want, if you put that need and desire out there, you'll find it does come to you: you'll 'discover' the perfect photo, or print, or poster in the unlikeliest of places, and you'll be on your way.

So that was the inside. Outside, I found the southeast corner of my property and created a 'prosperity garden.' I already had a forsythia bush in the southeast corner. Since this is a yellow flowering shrub, that worked. But after it leafs out and is green, I needed some yellow. And some water, yellow to signify gold coins and water to keep the Chi flowing.

I relocated a small birdbath to this spot: it's really just a spare saucer for under large pots, but it's quite deep and inside it I put a fairly heavy decorative bird feeder I'd never really used as such for fear it would get soiled. Then I filled this with sparkling clear water; I keep it full and clean out the dead leaves and other stuff that blows into it.

Alongside it I placed a couple of medium sized green planters. They're metal, which again strengthens the wealth aspect, and they look expensive even though they weren't. In them I planted bright yellow French marigolds that are round and remind me of gold coins. Every time I look at those marigolds, it's like a little intention: subconsciously I think 'prosperity' and the intention is made. The flowers last throughout the growing season and into the fall. During the winter I stuff the planters with holly sprigs and shiny gold holiday 'picks' with round ornaments that again resemble coins to carry forward the prosperity theme.

I have noticed a striking synchronicity with this prosperity garden, and also with the frog coin container, and my personal prosperity. All I have to do is to re-fill the birdbath, or change (or re position) the flowers in the planters and money arrives.

Immediately after I created my 'wealth corner' in my living space, I got a raise. I hadn't asked for it, wasn't even thinking about it, but my boss significantly increased my rate of pay.

Once, I moved the frog away from the prosperity corner for some reason, and some treasury bonds went missing. In a panic, I moved the frog back to where it had been (and where it still is) and a couple of days later, I found the bonds where they had been misplaced.

Another time, I changed the position of the planters with the yellow flowers in the garden, and a day or so later discovered my tax burden that year was much less than I'd anticipated. So the money I'd been saving for taxes wasn't needed--I bought new furniture with it.

Another time I cleaned out the bird bath and re-filled it, and the interest on a CD turned out to be thousands more than I'd anticipated--I gifted that in the form of paying for a friend's dream trip.

So there you have Vicki's story: a first hand account of what one person did and how things started to change. Like beginning with one item that when you look at it says 'prosperity' to you, you can begin small, with changes that cost nothing, or very little. But you will be amazed how fast things shift.

And speaking of shifting, that's the key: remember to shift how you view things first, in order to come from abundance.

If you're eating pasta four nights a week, try not to bemoan that fact. Try to remember that you are eating, nourishing your body, and get excited when you find a coupon for your favorite brand, or for a free jar of sauce. (And consider leaving a coupon for someone else, to 'share the wealth.')

If you're wearing hand me downs, you might want to look through every piece of clothing you own and think about removing anything that's really worn or faded (because that says 'poverty' not 'wealth'). Then consider that now you have room in your closet for clothes that really suit you and look good on you, and that you like. Until you have the money to go to the designer stores, pick up a shirt here or a sweater there, as long as they're in good condition, at yard sales or thrift shops: many of them might even boast 'designer' labels! One new item, or one different scarf, if you love it, is all it takes to build your wardrobe of wealth.

Once you have cleared room in the prosperity area of your living space, try not to look at the empty wall and think, 'I have nothing, it's so bare.' Instead, consider thinking, 'I've made room for things I love and for wealth to come in.'

And above all, Feng Shui teaches us to tend to our living areas, whether it's a room, a flat, or a house, a garden, a patio or just a window box. By clearing out the worn and caring for things we love, we automatically invite wealth in!

CHAPTER SEVEN

....

Reputation & Fame

South/Fire

THE SOUTH SECTION OF THE BAGUA is located opposite the front door. It is in the center of the back of the home or building according to BTB Feng Shui. You may refer to the Bagua map on the Frontispiece of this book to see this more clearly.

This is the area to focus on if you wish to increase your reputation and the recognition you receive in your chosen field, or if you wish to be famous. This is also the area in Feng Shui to focus on to raise the energy of your life and health, or personal and professional goals.

Colors in the red spectrum here are high vibration elements; along with candles, lamps and accent lighting of all kinds will raise the Chi or energy of this area substantially since this area resonates with the element of fire.

After 11 years studying and teaching Feng Shui and hearing continually from people that learning these techniques helped them understand and use Feng Shui simply and effectively, I know these techniques are important.

When I complete my annual goals, I include written present tense statements in small red envelopes and put them in the gua areas. These are called 'intention envelopes' and the statements are intentions. The envelopes may be placed in any segment of the Bagua where specific goals need enhancement. These envelopes were developed in BTB Feng Shui for the enhancement of aspirations.

In 2010 I wrote in my intention for the fame area that I was an internationally-known writer on Feng Shui; this is my story as to how this manifested in a very surprising way.

Sybilla's Story:

It was late June when I was driving my car, returning from an appointment when suddenly my heart started racing in my chest so fast I could not catch my breath, and had to pull over to the side of the road. I forced myself to slow my breath down and took deep calming breaths trying to steady my racing heart. After about five minutes, I felt I was able to pull back out on the road, but I was still very shaken.

Ten miles on, my heart jumped in my chest again and started racing once more. Now, I was really scared. I tried to calm myself down but I couldn't catch my breath. My heart was racing over 200 beats a minute and would not slow down.

By the time I was able to pull over once again and call an ambulance, my arms and hands were numb, and so was my chin. I was terrified. I felt my life was in jeopardy and I decided that I did not want to die, not until I had lived the rest of my life!

I was taken to the hospital and later had surgery to try to remedy the problem with my heart. The surgery was very tough and very uncomfortable.

I had a great deal of pain before and after, and to make matters worse, I really disliked my hospital room.

However, I came home from the hospital, but suffered that entire summer with irregular heartbeats. Finally, another event took place where my heart began beating so fast I couldn't catch my breath, and once again I was rushed to the hospital. Once again, I was told I would have to have surgery, and this time I was devastated and more fearful than ever.

While waiting for surgery, I chose to put some prayers out there for guidance because I had so much fear, and had had such a bad experience with the first surgery. That guidance came to me a few evenings later in the form of an email from a Hospital Administrator in India.

He had found my online Feng Shui site, and in his email, he asked if I would be willing to co-author a book about healing in hospitals.

I was astounded. Then I thought, "what a sign from above!" I had never considered that I might encourage my own healing in the hospital both before and after my first surgery, and I had never thought about any of the Feng Shui techniques I could use to make a difference in my own comfort. But once I read that email, I realized that Feng Shui could make a difference, and I agreed to submit a chapter on Feng Shui's rôle in hospitals and healing.

This was a great distraction during the next few weeks while I waited for the second surgery on my heart. It also made me pay attention to details for my own upcoming hospital stay.

One of the things I started to do right away was to visualize in my morning meditation a healthy and perfect outcome for the surgery. My intention was stronger than ever. I wanted to heal my heart and I was willing to do whatever it took for that to happen.

I started by re-examining the inside of my home in the center area that governs health. What needed to change? The artwork on the stairwell? The items on the shelf? Was it clean and clear? I decided the area could use a thorough cleaning. I also changed the artwork, adding some paintings *with red in them. Red is an energizer, and represents fire. Fire feeds earth and earth energy resonates with the center of a home or building.*

I cleaned the shelf, too, and added mineral geodes and crystals here, again to boost the earth element. It looked and felt good. Then I decided that in addition to the visualization I did each morning, I needed to assemble a 'care package' for my stay in the hospital.

I packed a cozy shawl to wrap up in while waiting in the pre-surgical area. I packed rose essential oil to dot on myself because the smell always makes me feel contented and loved. I brought music and artwork for my hospital room during my stay. I also did a mini space clearing in my room to help move on any stagnant energy from previous patients.

I was ready.

The surgery went off perfectly and painlessly and my hospital stay was comfortable, and even enjoyable!

Because of this episode in my life, my chapter on Feng Shui is included in the book <u>Designing Hospitals of the Future.</u> It is a beautifully illustrated book on how the design both inside and outside a hospital can assist in promoting health for those in need. It is now being circulated in India and Asia, and will soon be promoted here in the U.S.

I am honored to have been a part of such a wonderful project and I smile now, when I recall the power of intention and Feng Shui. I had placed the intention envelope in the South sector behind a piece of artwork, and never would have guessed the manner in which my intention would become manifest.

When scrutinizing the south area of your home or building, don't forget to look at the land outside this area too. Things to focus on for raising Chi in the south gua include adding lights and planting red flowers.

Inside, clean and de-clutter then space clear as always, and then take a look at what is in this section. Is it something you love to look at? Is the paint a color you like? Is there adequate lighting? If there is art, what does it say to you?

Be careful not to get carried away with too much red color here: fire is a very powerful element, and you may produce more energy than you are prepared for. Ideally, the area should be balanced with an additional boost from the fire element. This can be achieved with a fireplace or candles, lighting, artwork with red touches, and triangular shaped things.

If adding fire energy in this area doesn't work, remember you can also employ features that enhance the wood energy, since wood 'feeds' fire. Plants, pictures or paintings of plants or trees, the color green and similar features will all work.

CHAPTER EIGHT

Love & Relationships

Southwest/Earth

THIS SECTION OF THE GUA IS LOCATED in the far right corner of your home or building. You may refer to the Bagua map on the Frontispiece of this book to see this more clearly. This area is known for enhancing loving relationships or drawing loved ones into your life. The predominant element for the area is earth, which can be represented by colors of beige, yellow and brown. Earth is also represented by square shapes. Some Feng Shui masters consider shapes to be more powerful than the element itself.

If you wish to increase loving relationships in your life, you will want to thoroughly clean and de-clutter this area. Look for anything that is old, outdated or worn out. It is important to do this because everything in our environment is energetically connected to us in some way. In order to invite new, fresh energies in, we want to clear out, clean and repair the area.

The following story is an example of how attention to this gua and its energy manifested itself in one woman's life.

Michelle's Story:

. . . .

About five years ago, Michelle contacted me for her first Feng Shui consultation. After our initial introduction, we sat down in her living room. It was a cozy condominium space with a living room, bathroom, eat in kitchen and laundry room on the first floor. On the second floor there was a master bedroom and bath, along with another spare bedroom. While we were seated in the living room we talked about the Bagua energy template used in BTB Feng Shui.

I explained that there are nine areas of aspirations in the Bagua, and that the template is a representation of the ancient I-Ching. I-Ching is a very ancient Eastern philosophical practice based on interpreting the elements we live in and the quality of balance (yin/yang) in our inner and external environments. The Bagua is laid over the floor plan to determine the focal areas a person wishes to cultivate or enhance.

As I explained this to Michelle, she quickly spoke up and said she was lonely, and wanted a real change in her life. She was interested in finding a new job and more importantly a loving partner with whom she could share her life.

She began to tell me about a previous partner whom she had been engaged to, and said she was having a hard time getting over their break up. I discussed with her the energy of things, and how they hold the energy of others and the energies of the space they were in. It was very important, therefore, to pay attention to any objects or items that had been theirs together. If Michelle really wanted to move on in her life, she needed to pack away or give away anything that might represent that past relationship. If the ex-fiancé had given her jewelry or other items it was important to remove these, at the very least putting them away in a separate container that was out of sight, because they held the energy of her former loved one and the energy of the former relationship.

At that moment, Michelle looked down to the pillow she was holding next to her stomach. It was a pretty neatly crocheted couch pillow. She said, "Oh my gosh, I hold this every evening while I watch television, and I wonder why I can't get him out of my mind!" Her ex-fiancé had given her that pillow. "I need to put this in the box with all the other things he gave me in the past," Michelle said.

We located the southwest gua in her home and I suggested that Michelle clear what she could out of that area, and give it a thorough cleaning and space clearing. Then I suggested she could bring in things in pairs, and things that signified loving relationships. I mentioned a pair of glass lovebirds, or artwork of couples together as being ideal for this area. Square shapes, signifying earth, and pink to signify love are also good touches here.

I also suggested that she add a second nightstand in her bedroom, not only to balance her bed, but also to spark the energy to attract a partner to share her life. The artwork above her bed, while beautiful, was a painting of a single person walking along a serene beach. I suggested Michelle move that somewhere else and replace it with a picture of a couple. Again, pairs of things in a bedroom, regardless of what area of the house it is in, helps to boost the 'couple 'energy. So if this is what you want in your life, it is a good thing to employ this technique.

In the southwest area of her home, Michelle placed a lovely piece of rose quartz near a pair of glass lovebirds. Then she went through all her belongings and furniture and eliminated everything that represented anyone from her past.

Three months later, Michelle contacted me with great news. She said she could not believe the power Feng Shui had unleashed in her life. She told me she had been offered, and taken, a new job in her chosen field. The job was four hours away from her old condominium, so she had moved.

But then she told me that while working in the new city, she had met a wonderful man and was happier than she had ever been.

Another story illustrates the way in which enhancing the relationship area of the Bagua can help attract a wonderful partner.

Teresa's Story:
....

A woman contacted me who was in her mid 70's. She had read articles and seen snippets of stories about Feng Shui on television and wanted to have a consultation. She mentioned in our first meeting that she had been widowed for over 20 years and felt very lonely.

Teresa was a very energetic woman and felt she had a lot of years left; she did not want to live the remainder of her life alone.

She had a very neat and orderly home. As we went through it, I made a few suggestions here and there. But then we came to her bedroom. As is common among single people, the bedroom was set up for one occupant. It was also decorated in stark white, with a single night stand, closets completely full of her clothing, pictures of her children, books, and a television next to the bed on the side where she slept.

I explained to Teresa that while it's nice to have pictures of your children, they are best in a different area of the home, such as the east, which governs family. Also, having books and a television in the bedroom are distracting to the occupant and strengthen the atmosphere of solitary pursuits and interests.

Bedrooms are meant to be quiet, calm, balanced spaces to promote good and restorative sleep for the mind and body. Distractions like a television and many books are better placed elsewhere. Additionally, if the person wants to have a partner in life, the bedroom space should be made welcoming so that the energy of a partner may find its way there.

Teresa made it clear that she wasn't interested in remarriage or a live in relationship, but would very much like a companion to share dinners, movies, and other pursuits. I explained to her that by tweaking a few things in her bedroom she would invite exactly the sort of companion she wanted.

I suggested, as I had with Michelle, that she add a second nightstand to balance the bed and boost the 'couple' energy. When Teresa told me she had a hard time sleeping, I encouraged her to move the television away from the bed, and to cover it with a pretty cloth when it wasn't in use: this would contain the television's natural energy.

Teresa had a large mirror in the bedroom as well, and I explained that the mirror reflected the room's Chi or energy. While this is good, in a bedroom it can be very distracting and not conducive to rest. I suggested she cover the mirror at night to see if she felt better and slept better.

Helping Teresa feel calmer and more rested would also encourage a loving relationship because she would be more receptive.

I heard back from Teresa in a few months. She had taken many of my suggestions and was happy to report that she had been introduced to a wonderful elderly gentleman who had been looking for a dancing partner. He was 17 years her senior, but so far, they are still having dinner and dancing the night away every Friday!

And finally, a third story about creating the relationship you want with the assistance of Feng Shui.

Siobhan's Story:

After spending almost ten years trying to understand my life and my own patterns of behavior I heard about Feng Shui. I read that applying the ancient principles of Feng Shui could help a person attract the perfect loving relationship. I had always wanted to have the right mate in my life, but could not seem to attract that perfect partner, so I decided to give Feng Shui a try.

My consultation began by placing the Bagua energy template over my home's floor plan. This showed that the southwest corner governing relationships was in my kitchen, so that was the area I needed to work on.

My Feng Shui master explained that the entire window over the kitchen sink should be cleaned out and cleared of all items. This would keep the window clear so that the Chi could flow easily. My kitchen was painted a light mauve; adding pink and red would enhance the element native to this gua, which is earth. I added a red vase that was shaped like a heart, and I put a note nearby of what I wanted my partner to be like. I added a picture of a loving couple here too.

Then I went to my bedroom, located the southwest corner of the room itself, and applied some of the same principles in that area. I placed a picture in that corner of two swans, and a lovely figurine of swans entwined; swans mate for life. Beneath the figurine I placed my intention envelope and inside I wrote my aspiration for a loving and permanent relationship.

My treadmill happened to be in this corner of the bedroom, so I put pictures next to it of a log home in the woods, something I had always longed for, and a picture of a diamond engagement ring to symbolize a happy and romantic union. Every time I exercised, I looked at these pictures, and I visualized a wonderful romance and my dream home and partner.

Within a year, a friend of mine stopped by my office and told me she wanted me to meet someone special. "He's a builder," she told me. "I just have a really strong feeling you two should meet." She gave him my name and he called me. We met for breakfast and instantly 'clicked,' talking like we were old friends.

He was a builder, yes, but he specialized in LOG HOMES! He was a widower, and a wonderful family man, and it was easy for me to fall in love with him. Within six months we were engaged, and a year later we were married. We now live in...a log home in the woods.

I believe that the positive powers of visualization, intention, and using the natural energies through the principles of Feng Shui helped me find true and lasting happiness with the perfect partner.

·······················

Creativity & Children

West/Metal

THE TOPICS OF CREATIVITY AND CHILDREN are in the same chapter because both types of creations come from a person's body, spirit, and intellect. In fact, artists--whether authors, painters, or musicians--often speak of their books, paintings and songs as their 'children,' metaphorically if not directly.

If you are seeking fulfillment and success in a creative endeavor whether it is your avocation or your profession, or if you wish to have 'children' in the more usual sense of the word (whether adopted or biologically yours), or if you want to improve your relationship with your children, you will want to pay attention to the creativity/children corner of your home. This area of the home connects with the passionate creative aspect of life.

The west governs this aspect, and the colors and elements linked with this area are yellows and creams, and metal. The metal can be silver, gold or anything in between! You may refer to the Bagua map on the Frontispiece of this book to see this more clearly.

As always, look at this area critically and think about what you have or do that is creative. If you are a musician, the west is a great spot to locate your 'music room,' or keep your instruments, music, etc. If you paint or do any sort of physical creating including pottery, mixed media, weaving--you get the idea--this is the area in your home where, if you can, it would be ideal for you to set up your studio. If you write, here's the spot to build your study.

If you wish to start a family, this area is where you would want to put pictures of that energy: pictures of children, things that suggest pregnancy like paintings of round fruits, and convex mirrors. Some very suggestive prints, which may be subtly erotic to you but not to everyone, could also go here.

Every time you look at these paintings, these items, they speak to the creative element within you. They become, in fact, talismans, and as such they reinforce and reiterate your intention.

Now that you've begun to visualize that area as you want it to be, clear it out to make room for the things you want to put there. Look at this as an opportunity to re-arrange and stir up the Chi: not only will you sparkle that creativity area, you'll refresh the Chi in your entire house! Not to mention the fact that you'll have a good clean as well.

If you can, take away all the furniture and wall decor presently in this space. Clean it, then paint or wallpaper this section or room in a soft yellow, cream, beige, etc. You may wish to burn incense, light candles, or use another space clearing technique such as hand clapping or bell ringing to thoroughly clear the space. Then bring in the items you visualized as making up your creative space. Bring elements into the area that are in the cream-yellow-beige color spectrum. Also remember to bring in metallics: gold, silver, etc.

Gracie's story:

I'm a writer and a newspaper reporter. Recently I began learning about Feng Shui and I had a Feng Shui Consultant come and critique my house. We talked, of course, about the status of my career: it's going well, but could be better.

One thing she mentioned was that my desk should face west; at the moment it faces east, and is on the east side of the room. Having it in the west would take advantage of the natural creative Chi in that area.

My reply was 'but that's where the phone line is, and I need to have the phone on my desk and I need the phone line to connect to the internet.'

She smiled in that Mona Lisa way many wise people have and we moved on to other things.

Months later, having seen a lot of changes because of other aspects of Feng Shui that I'd attended to, my thoughts returned to the question of where to put my desk. Since our initial consultation, the main reason (or excuse) for keeping the desk where I'd located it has evaporated: I no longer use the telephone to connect to the internet. So my desk can really be located anywhere I choose. What freedom!

Oddly enough, when I write, whether it's an article for the newspaper or one of my novels, I rarely actually sit at my desk. I almost always sit on the couch--facing WEST.

So I've decided to move rather a lot of furniture and to re-locate my desk and printer against the west wall of the 'great room,' facing west. It will mean moving pictures and paintings, too, though thankfully the wall is already a creamy beige.

One of the best things is that in doing this move I will actually open up a space in the area of the room where my desk now is and be able to have something I've always wanted but never thought I had the room for: one of those entry/foyer 'trees' with the coat hooks, bench and mirror. This spot is also adjacent to the front door of my house, so this piece of furniture will be perfect there.

The thing I've learned, once again, is that if you open up to the possibilities of the natural Chi in your home, not only will you successfully take advantage of the energy's resonances, you may also achieve something else you've wanted but weren't consciously working on, at the same time!

And as for how this shift has affected my career, I'm still in the planning stages although the decision has been made. Just this morning I received a huge boost to my first book, published two weeks ago: enthusiastic comments by a well known author who (without my asking) put her review on the internet, and mentioned my book on her website!

Paul's Story:

I'm a musician, and after I had some success my wife and I bought a large historic home out in the country. I had a music room purpose-built and now that I think back about it (although I no longer live there), it was in the western corner of the house!

When I moved several years later, I bought a condominium that had a glorious view, and faced south, though I didn't think about directions at the time, just the view. Once again, I wanted to create a music room, where I could compose, work on songs, and keep my instruments and memorabilia.

The problem was, the flat had three bedrooms, with a rather large master bedroom facing south and west, and a balcony running the full length of the outside, and massive windows. I wanted to have my music room where I could see that amazing view! And I kept gravitating towards the room intended as a master bedroom.

But that didn't seem practical, so I used one of the guest bedrooms as my music room instead. However, it never felt 'right.' I was also hesitant to use it because, even with soundproofing, the room shared a common wall with my neighbor across the hall, and I didn't imagine they'd want to hear, even faintly, my musical noodling at all hours of the night!

This was around the time I became acquainted with a woman in my new community who knew about Feng Shui, and she confirmed my intuition that I should have my music room in the west facing area of my new flat. This was also around the time I realized the music room in my former home had in fact been in the west of the house. I had had a great deal of success professionally, and a lot of satisfaction from the music I wrote in that room and I wanted to re-create that experience where I now lived.

I tried to convince myself, and my friend, that the smaller of the two guest bedrooms was fine as my new music room: it was in the west, after all, so it should be suitable. It had a window, but by comparison not a very large one, and no balcony, and the common wall issue still concerned me.

As all of this was going on, and it was a process of a few years, I continued to write music but I didn't have as much success as I had before. It was rather a depressing time for me with a lot of upset, and although I still wrote, I felt that a lot of what I was writing was at the worst not very good and at the best, hard won. And although I found a lot of 'reasons' for my lack of success that had nothing to do with the placement of my music room--economic downturn, personnel changes, the natural ebb and flow of a career--it still bothered me that the music room didn't feel 'right.'

The fact was, I never actually wrote in that room. I always took my guitar into my bedroom--the master suite--and sat on the bed (facing west) and wrote, or went out on the balcony and wrote (again, facing west). When I checked into it, most of the really successful songs, and all of the ones I like the best, have all been written facing west, no matter where I was.

I finally gave in to my nagging feeling, and brought in an architect who was able to carve out a space from the west end of the master suite and part of the second guest room and build a totally west-facing music room for me. I still have the guest room, but it's a proper guest room now. I still have a master bedroom, too, and it's still quite spacious. But I also have my wonderful music room, soundproofed but in no danger of bothering the neighbors with any noise, and with a door opening off the master suite and off the hallway. There's plenty of room for everything, and most of all, those wonderful huge western windows and balcony, that evocative western view that I find so inspiring.

Strangely enough, my career has begun to take an upward turn since completing this construction, and more importantly I feel that the music I'm writing is some of the best I ever have.

Carina's story:

I had been married very young and had a child who at the time of my second marriage--the first ended in divorce--was 18 and on his own. My second marriage was to a man who had also been married and divorced, but he had never had children. We both wanted to have at least one child together. For many reasons, we felt we had each found our 'soulmate,' the perfect person we were meant to be with.

I was 36 at the time of my second marriage. We tried for four years to have children, including fertility drugs and very expensive IVF therapy that took a good chunk of my husband's savings. We had all the tests but nothing seemed conclusive: according to my doctors, I should have been pregnant after a few months of 'trying' at the most.

I'm an accountant and just after my 40th birthday, when John and I had more or less given up on having a family of our own, I got a new client: a man who was a Feng Shui 'master.' I found myself intrigued by his business. I looked Feng Shui up on the internet and discovered some amazing claims. Although I didn't really believe what people said about how Feng Shui changed their lives, I wondered if, somehow, Feng Shui could help me.

I talked it over with John, who, as I had expected, was very leery of the idea at first. I tried to explain what I'd read online and stressed that it was about opening up your life to good energy, and moving out the bad stuff.

'So it's changing the furniture around?' he asked. I told him, yes, but it's more than that.

Finally, he asked me what it would cost. I had contacted my client, the one whose taxes I do, and found out from him that for an initial visit/consultation, and a follow up visit/recommendation/explanation, it would cost $250.

John smiled when I told him that. 'Go ahead, if it will make you happy,' he said. 'We've spent a lot more than that, so if that's all it costs, I'm all for it.'

To make a long story short, I met with my client: he came to our house and on the spot told me a few things, but when he returned with my Bagua Map and his analysis and recommendations, I really had to get to work.

My creativity section in the west was on one end of our living room; we own an historic house from the 1850's and in those days it was the fashion to have two front doors off a common porch that ran along the front of the house. One of our front doors leads into a little foyer, and then to a dining room and stairs to go up to the second floor. We mostly use the back door, but that front door is the one we use. The other one was on the end of the living room and we had put a sofa and end tables up against it, and covered the glass panes in the door with a shade and floor length curtains.

It took a couple of weeks, and I did several other things in other areas of the house, but the first thing I did was move all the furniture around in the living room, taking the sofa and end tables away from the west wall and opening up the door. The shade and curtain came down. I put a large mirror and a coat rack on one side of the door, and a small armchair and table on the other side of the door to create a foyer like space. I also bought a round area rug in shades of yellow and cream to pull this area together. Beyond it was the rest of the living room with the sofa and end tables--now in a much better spot opposite the entertainment center--more chairs, etc.

I also painted that west wall of the living room a deep creamy yellow color. The rest of the living room was beige and one wall was brick, so it looked okay. I moved some pictures we had had in our bedroom down to flank the doorway: they were pictures of peonies, my favorite flowers, but their round shape was good and the colors were right.

The biggest change I made was the door itself: I scrubbed the windows and painted the door that same deep creamy yellow inside, to match the walls. And I started using that door when I entered and left the house, even though it meant walking the length of the porch and around the side of the house to the back drive where I kept my car.

Spring came, and John put in a walkway along the side of the house. We took an early vacation to a local beach and he brought his camera along and got a really nice shot of some children feeding seagulls. Back home I had it made into a poster, framed it, and hung it on the wall next to the west door along with my peony watercolors. All were framed in a brushed silver and I found when I came and went through that door, I smiled, and I thought about the nurturing side of myself and creative ways I could share that whether or not I ever had children of my own.

That September, I registered with the local school system and became a Math Tutor. I'd always loved math, which is why I became an accountant. I had three students almost right away: two girls and a boy, all between 8-11 years old.

It had been seven months since I'd made my major Feng Shui changes in my house, and I still used that western front door all the time, but I'd begun to 'chalk it up to experience' and feel that although the money had been well spent and I liked the changes to my home, I was just too old to have children by now.

I talked it over with John, and he reluctantly agreed. The room next to ours that we had intended for a nursery would become something else, we decided--in the winter time, when we were indoors more and could devote ourselves to a DIY project.

It's a good thing we waited, because by Christmas that year I was pregnant. With twins. And as I write this, they are two months old, healthy, happy, and wanting a feeding!

Let me just say that for me Feng Shui is about opening up--literally--yourself to possibilities and then enjoying what you have already in your life. While I made my intention and thought about children every time I looked at that new front door, I also didn't stay trapped as I had been in longing. That isn't coming from abundance, which was another lesson I learned. I tried to be open to many different interpretations of motherhood and start to bring those into my life, still wanting children of my own, but finding my nurturing mother-self nonetheless.

So there you have it: stories by very different people who wanted to achieve success in the different aspects of the creative mode and who took advantage of the natural creative Chi that is so abundant in the western area.

Not only that, you can see from their stories that two of these three people had a natural 'instinct' about the direction that turned out to be the best for their creativity! Learn to trust your instincts.

In Feng Shui, elements always have complements: in this case, the element metal in the west is complemented by earth energy. You can boost the energy of the metal frames and objects you place in the western part of your living space by also using stones, crystals, marble, terra cotta. The element that blocks or draws away from the creative energy in this case is fire, so avoid triangular objects and colors from the red spectrum in this area.

As always, go with your instincts once you have informed your mind: if something really speaks to you, inspires you, and it happens to be red or triangular, by all means go ahead and include it in this new creative space. Your personal talismans are important, and Chi is, after all, fluid.

....

Helpful People & Travel

Northwest/Metal

THE NORTH WEST AREA OF YOUR LIVING SPACE is the one devoted to helpful people and travel. This includes spirit guides or people who are important influences in your life as well as places you have been or wish to go. It also involves communication. If you are planning to move, or wish to move, enhance this space to make the move an easy one.

The color here is grey and the element is metal. You may refer to the Bagua map on the Frontispiece of this book to see this more clearly.

The most important thing about this area is, even more so than other areas of your living space, to keep it open and uncluttered, welcoming, so the spirit guides and helpful people can come in to assist you. Also, the energy of travel and communication needs space to occupy: try not to clutter up your north west corner to impede that.

As always, clear away everything that's in this space and clean it. If you can, paint the walls a silvery grey tone, nothing dark or depressing. Failing that, keep the walls white and introduce elements in greys and silvers to enhance the natural Chi there.

Also you might want to repair anything broken in this area: small window panes, screens, moulding: it would be best to have it all fixed and in good order before you begin re-decorating.

If you want more travel, place images relating to travel in this area: maps, photos of places you want to go, memorabilia of where you've been (and want to return). This is not a bad place to have your TV and/or satellite dish (outside), since both bring the world to you, as it were.

If you want to attract helpful people, whether corporeal or spiritual, this is the spot for figurines or paintings of angels and spirit guides. You could also put pictures in this area of ancestors with whom you feel a special resonance, or even photos of people who have been important in your life, who have influenced you.

Use whites, greys, and blacks as your decor elements and incorporate metal when possible.

When you look at or spend time in this area of your living space, you want to be able to reflect on the places you've been, think about the places you wish to go, and communicate with entities who can help you enhance all aspects of your life.

Jean's Story:

When I bought my new bungalow, I decided that the room directly next to my front entry hall would be my guest room. It could have been my bedroom, but I chose a room at the center of the house for my bedroom. I painted the walls of the guest room white and hung blue curtains with a white paisley motif, and chose white furniture for the room. I had a large cupboard type of armoire built against one wall and in here I keep my computer and a lot of reference books.

In the guest room, which is north west, I also keep most of my CD and DVD collection. I also have a couple of autographed photos of actors or musicians I've admired, framed and hung on these walls.

I had very little money when I moved in, having just come out of a divorce, and it was a point in my life when I was just grateful to have a home of my own and a decent job. But I also longed for adventure, and travel. However, my income didn't stretch to that, so I decorated the walls of my new home, and especially of this guest room, with pictures I picked up at jumble sales and thrift stores. They were always pictures of places I wanted to go. I had grown up during the end of the Second World War, and had always loved airplanes, so photographs of many planes also found their way into this room. And I spent many hours in this room at my computer, virtually visiting all sorts of places all over the world and out into space--I am quite fond of space and physics and make no apologies for liking science fiction.

Only about a year after I had moved, actually less than that, I made some new friends from the US, a place I had always wanted to visit and never dreamt I would. They came to visit me, staying in my guest room. I added a couple of pictures of the US to the walls, and one of these friends--although I am still friends with them all-- within another year had become one of the best friends I've ever had in my life. She is such a good friend, and visits so often, that she keeps a backup wardrobe and toiletries in what we all refer to as 'her' room, now!

When she visits, she rents a car and we drive all over England. We've gone up to Scotland and down to Hastings, and made many many visits to nearly every county in England. I have seen more of my own country since she has been in my life than ever before.

I have also been fortunate enough to visit the US not just once, but five times in the past several years, and see places I had pictures of on my guest rooms walls but had never expected or hoped to visit: the Grand Canyon, New York, Boston, Washington D.C., even Louisiana's bayous and Texas. I even got to go to NASA!

When this same friend learned about Feng Shui she did a fast analysis of my home and one of the things that struck both of us was the placement and decoration of my guest room and the things that have happened since moving here and creating that space.

Apparently, without knowing a single thing about Feng Shui I instinctively created a space in the right spot of my new home that would bring me visitors, and enable me to travel far beyond anything I'd ever done before or ever imagined I'd do.

I am amazed, and I am also keeping the guest room in the same place and decorated the same way, despite some recent renovations to the inside of my home.

When my friend visits next, she says she will help me adjust the rest of my house to take advantage of the good energies naturally occurring there. If it does half of what that guest room has done for my life, I'll be forever grateful!

Anna and Bob's Story:

Anna: We inherited our house from Bob's family. Over the years it's been added onto, porches have been put on, enclosed, etc. until it has become quite large. Mostly everyone comes in our 'back' door, which leads into the kitchen.

Our front door, which faces in the same direction as the 'back' door, is part of the original house dating from the 1890's. Few people use it, but we keep it in working order nonetheless.

It opens directly into a large area we now use as a dining room and the right hand wall is the north west section of our house.

Although with the deaths of parents and grandparents we have inherited everything from an antique doll collection to a miniature pipe organ, we have always kept pictures and mementos of our ancestors in that area.

For me, it is a reminder whenever I look at it that people who have gone before me but who loved me very much, or who have loved my husband, are watching over me.

Bob: Although I agree with what my wife says, when I look at those pictures and belongings from her ancestors or mine, I feel a deep sense of solidarity and a sense of history. I am reminded of my place in this world and in this community and the family into which I was born and into which we have brought our own children and now grandchildren.

We are always renovating the house, since a house over 100 years old always is in need of something. When the time comes to re-paint that section of the house, I'd consider using a soft dove grey color to enhance the energy.

Anna: At Christmas, we always put our angel statue in that corner, too, on top of a large desk that used to belong to Bob's great grandfather. When I look at her I think of all the blessings we have in this life, in some part because of the work of those who went before us.

Once again, both of these stories tell of people who instinctively knew how to take advantage of the natural energy in the north west corner of their living spaces. Imagine how effective one could be if one made some simple changes to work with the Chi!

Whether it's helpful people in this life or helpful people who have passed on; whether you're an armchair traveler through computer or TV, or one actually racking up frequent flyer miles; whether it's people or places who inspire and energize you: the north west corner of your home is the place for them.

Try some simple moves, changes, enhancements here, and see if you don't discover more mentors, friends, travel and adventure coming your way!

CHAPTER ELEVEN

....

Mind, Body & Spirit

Center/Earth

IF YOU HAVE READ THE PREVIOUS CHAPTERS OF THIS BOOK, you probably feel as though you have learned a great deal in a short while. At least, we hope you feel that way!

Sometimes it can be difficult to 'keep it all together,' particularly when you are being exposed to a lot of new ideas, people, places, etc.

We have, in the previous chapters, traveled around your living space through the sections of the Bagua, but now it is time to center ourselves and visit the middle of your living space. This resonates with one's mind, body and spirit and how they interact, and relates to the state of one's mental and physical health. You may refer to the Bagua map on the Frontispiece of this book to see this more clearly.

Most people would agree that human beings are made up of both mental and physical attributes: the mind and the body, if you will.

A good portion, though not all, would agree that there is a third element to humans. Whether you want to call it 'soul' or 'emotion' or 'compassion' or 'spirit,' which is the term we use, this element differs from the intellect/mind element and the body element because not only does it stand alone, it enhances, informs and connects the other two.

The center portion of your home is the part that resonates with the core of your being: your spirit, mind and body. All three must work together just as in the center of your living space you must have harmonious items and things that bring the energy of earth. Earth is the element associated--logically--with the center. Although Earth is the predominant element here, the center is also where all the elements join together. So you may feel free to incorporate aspects of the other elements (fire, water, metal, wood) in the central area.

The center of your home may be a room, or a staircase, or even a closet! No matter what it is, follow the same path we have taken in other areas: clean and clear away, then re-populate with items connected to the specific energy or Chi of the space.

In this case, once you have cleaned and cleared--and here's that opportunity to get rid of the clutter in that closet!--incorporate paint or wall covering in earth tones: beiges, browns, yellows. Fire 'feeds' earth, so bring in red, gold, pink, even purple tones as long as it's not too blue. Whatever you have in the center should be things you love, things you enjoy looking at, using or having.

If your home's center is a room, regardless of the function of that room, be sensitive to the flow of Chi and recognize that the architects who built your house may not have had the principles of Feng Shui in mind. Create, if you can, a tranquil yet empowered space utilizing the earth tone and fire tone palettes. If there are windows, be sure to use shades, blinds or curtains: you want to let light in, of course, but you also don't want the Chi to be unconfined. Heavy dark drapes are not appropriate, however.

Once you make your walls an earth color, place pictures, ornaments and other items that invoke or have a correspondence with the earth element: landscapes, collections of rocks or stones or crystals, decorative objects that bring you comfort, happiness and a feeling of fulfillment and serenity. Keep the area clear of clutter and again, be sure everything, in this area especially, is something you really like. (This is not the room for the vase Great Aunt Myrtle gave you that you despise but feel you ought to display somewhere!)

If your space's center is a closet, needless to say, clean it out, keep it tidy, and make sure that nothing gets lost back in the corners or under things. This closet, like the room, represents the heart of your living space. It should bring you joy, comfort, and a feeling of security. Keep it tidy. (One friend I know has a linen closet in this space and has it organized by color and fabric so when you open the door, it's like looking at a rainbow!)

If the center of your home is a staircase, you may have to work a little harder to create a feeling of 'security' because a stairway by definition is not a resting point but a place of movement.

However, this is one of the most interesting aspects for Feng Shui and it's also quite common. Many houses have a stairway in their center; properly decorated and enhanced, a central stairway can not only remind you of the sturdiness of your home (and therefore, of security), it can also be a metaphorical link between levels of consciousness. Like mind and body making up the intellectual and corporeal parts of a human being, levels of a home work together, but also separately. And, like 'spirit,' the staircase is not only a thing in and of itself, it is also the link between the other levels or aspects.

If you are lucky enough to have a stairway at the center of your house, again, follow the clean and de-clutter strategy and then the space clearing ritual; then bring in paint, carpet and decorative touches that resonate: earth tones and fire tones. Be wary of storing things on the stairs: it may be convenient, but it impedes the flow of Chi and defeats the purpose of the stairway, to move people and energy between floors.

Do decorate the wall or walls surrounding your staircase, unless it's a freestanding one. (Even then, you may wish to have mobiles hanging, crystals, etc.) Again, think about using pictures and decorative elements that you love in this area, and in addition to the landscapes and crystals mentioned before when discussing a room at the center of the living space, if your center is a staircase, you may also incorporate anything that brings to mind that 'other' element of spirit or soul. Transcendent yantras, pictures of diversity in concord, and most of all things you really love all belong here.

One person we know keeps all her metaphysical books on one shelf in the stairwell, and on the other she keeps books she loves that she never wants to part with. These choices are perfect because the metaphysical of course, treats transcendence and moving between the states or planes of being. And for this woman, who is a writer, keeping books she loves in this space speaks to her inner core, and links the core of her home to the core of her self.

Nyada's story:
....

The house I grew up in had a strange square hallway in its center. There were five doors off this hallway, doors to two bedrooms, a bathroom, a kitchen and a dining room. The space also had a sixth door, for a linen closet. The hallway itself was not very big: about 30 square feet and if we shut all the doors it was totally dark unless we turned on the overhead light.

As a young girl I remember being very unsettled, very active, but not because I was a tomboy by nature, more because of a restlessness that seemed to always be in the background of my life. I believe, now that I know a little bit about Feng Shui, that restlessness was due in part to the fact that my living space, my home, contained at its core that funny square hallway with all the doors. The center of my childhood home was not a place of peace, serenity, quiet or satisfaction. Instead, it was constantly in motion with people rushing through it as they went into and out of the rooms opening into it. To make things worse, my mother hung a full length mirror on the only wall space big enough to accommodate one. I now realize that the Chi was constantly racing around this space at the core of my house, never settling, never resting.

I wish I could tell you that we solved this issue, but I don't think anyone recognized what was at the heart of the matter. We did, however, move only a few years after moving in to that house and our new home, which I liked much better, held no such peculiar construction. I felt much more content in the new house, did better in school because my concentration was improved and was overall a happier child.

I do remember, though, loving to play in that funny hall when I was a little kid. But first--and this was crucial--I would always shut all the doors. Although it was pitch black in my 'playroom' then, a flashlight solved that, and I could feel, immediately, the energy in the room settle down. I, too, relaxed, and played.

Although there may not be a very practical solution to the crazy Chi Nyada had at the core of her childhood home, had her family recognized what was going on, there were measures they could have taken that would have helped. Nyada remembers the walls in the hall were pink and the carpet was an oriental in tones of red yellow and black. Painting the hallway beige and/or changing the carpet to a solid one in an earth tone would have helped considerably.

Also, replacing the mirror with a landscape or wall hanging/tapestry in earth tones would have helped. Small pictures in a similar vein on other walls of the hall would have been a good idea too.

Keeping the door to the bathroom closed would have vastly improved the situation, and the door to the dining room--which itself also opened onto the living room and had a door to the kitchen--could easily have also stayed shut most of the time.

That would have toned down the energy in the hallway, and meant only three doors into and out of it; both of the doors to the bedrooms could also have been partially shut to further contain the Chi.

Once again, treat the center of your home, whether it be a hall, a room or a stairway, as you do the rest of your living space as regards Feng Shui: clean it, and keep it tidy. Think about removing things you don't like from this space, and either finding a place where you do like them or having a jumble sale. Be certain there are no 'blocks' to the energy in this space, but don't make it so the energy bounces off walls and rushes through doors. Bring in things you love, keeping in mind the idea of mind/body/spirit.

Use earth tones highlighted by fire tones. And keep the area well lit but not too bright.

The center of your living space is aligned metaphysically with the core of yourself. As such it should be balancing, steadying and pleasing all at the same time. A hallway or a room can be decorated to achieve this effect and while a staircase is a bit more challenging, it too can be transformed from just a way to go between floors. A central stair can become a spot where one lingers to look at favorite pictures or decorative items, or beloved books. It can also be a subtle reminder that at our core is our heart, our spirit, which, like the stairway, flows between the levels of our selves, enabling communication back and forth and connecting everything into one integrated whole.

CHAPTER TWELVE

....

Gardening

The Outdoor Bagua

IT IS SAID IN FENG SHUI that the land is more important than the house, and the house is more important than the occupants. Why?

Beautiful gardens are created in Asia by establishing small mountains, ponds, and shrubs and trees to mimic the larger landforms in the surrounding areas. For centuries the most powerful rulers and members of the nobility demanded gardens like this. Why?

The reason is that by surrounding one's home with land forms that echo the natural geometry of the region, one encourages maximum Chi and abundance. Nobles and rulers employed Feng Shui masters who were expert in the art of aesthetics. They did intricate calculations to determine the path of Chi, and then determine how this would affect the people living and working in the palaces, homes and buildings.

In India, a type of Feng Shui called Vastu Shastra is used for similar purposes. The masters take precise measurements of the land to determine the flow of Chi, which in India is called 'Prana.' This is done before buildings or homes are even built. This is very important for all construction, but particularly for homes and hospitals where health and healing are so important.

The land is mounded and leveled to ensure an abundant and unimpeded flow of Chi or Prana into and out of the building. This has been done throughout Asia and the Indian sub-continent for thousands of years.

In <u>Designing Hospitals of the Future</u>, these philosophies of understanding and enhancing the flow of Chi are illustrated in practice. They have been proven to encourage healing and well being.

Let's take a look at the land outside of your home, apartment or condominium, and see how adding plants, trees, flowers and rocks can increase the Chi on your property and in your life.

The following guas explain the elements, colors and plants you may use to encourage and attract auspicious energy. You may refer to the Bagua map on the Frontispiece of this book to see this more clearly. The Outdoor Bagua is merely an extension of the Bagua placed over the floor plan of the inside of the home or building.

North: the element here is water. This is a perfect area outside for a water feature such as a birdbath, or small pond. You may have Koi or goldfish too if you like. If you can't put in a water feature, using flowers that are blue, white, and red will be great here too.

Northeast: the element here is earth. Using boulders, rocks, rock walls and other stone or rock features in the garden design is good here. Also, this is a good spot for yellow flowers or flowering shrubs and trees.

East: the element here is wood. Hedges or evergreen bushes and trees are perfect for this area.

Southeast: the element here is also wood, so again hedges and evergreens work well. You may also add a water feature of some kind because water 'feeds' wood energy. Flowers in purple, red and gold are great for enhancing the wealth aspiration here.

South: the element here is fire. Add brilliant red flowers or extra outdoor lighting to enhance the energy. This is also a good spot for outdoor grills, fire pits, chimineas and the like.

Southwest: the element here is earth. Use flowers in beiges and yellows, with pink here and feature terra cotta planters and garden ornaments if you have them.

West: the element here is metal. This is a perfect locale for wind chimes. White and yellow flowers work well here to boost the metal energy.

Northwest: the element here is metal again. It is said that multicolored flowers here will help attract helpful people or mentors, and promote travel. Metal lawn ornaments, or more wind chimes, work well here.

Center: this is ideally a fusion of all the elements, all in balance. If you are lucky enough to have a central garden focal point such as an atrium, adding anything earthen to resonate with the natural earth energy will be auspicious. Flowers would be best in the yellow spectrum, with other colors accenting.

In addition to that, certain flowers and plants in Feng Shui symbolize particular characteristics. These can be planted or placed in the areas of the outdoor Bagua where you might wish to enhance those characteristics.

Hydrangea symbolizes achievement. Therefore, hydrangeas might be good in the north gua, because north signifies career and life purpose.

Gardenias mean strength; they can be used in any gua where you feel the need to boost the energy.

Orchids signify endurance. These graceful and lovely plants can be very helpful in the northeast area because that relates to wisdom and self actualization. This is often a life long process, requiring endurance. However, if you are embarking on any kind of effort that you feel will require staying power, orchids in that gua can give it a boost.

Peonies mean wealth. While you could place them in the southeast, they will help usher in abundance regardless of where you locate them.

Pines especially mean longevity. It would be amazing to build your home around a huge pine tree, and thus have the center of your home be grounded in longevity. But it probably isn't practical. Instead, consider putting pines in the east, where family resonates, to help ensure long lives for all you hold near and dear.

Rhododendrons signify delicacy, sensitivity, and the quality of perceptiveness. These work well in the east to help promote harmony and understanding among family members. In the west, they could help do the same for children or for group creative projects where harmony is valued. Placed in the northeast, rhododendrons would help enhance one's own compassion and understanding.

As always, be mindful of the needs of the plants as you consider where you wish to place them. Some, like orchids, might best be used indoors unless you live in a tropical climate. Be sure to use plants outside that are appropriate for your hardiness zone.

Further, some plants need full sun, while others need shade; some may be more tender and need protection from wind. These considerations are important because you do not want to place a plant in a section of your outdoor Bagua to enhance that area, only to have the plant die or fail to thrive or bloom.

Understanding the subtle influences of plants, rocks, decorative elements, colors, and flowers will help you achieve an even larger personal Bagua that encompasses your entire property, and create and extend the harmonies and enhancements in all areas of your life.

CONCLUSION

The goal of this chapter is to give you thoughts and ideas to ponder, and to help you start a simple plan to take what you have learned in this book and apply it in a way you can use. Perhaps you will want to start by checking the pathway to your home and making sure it is unobstructed and as clean as possible.

One of the first things to do when you are readying yourself for your Feng Shui consultation is to examine the perimeter of your property and scrutinize the shape of the land surrounding your property. Are there mountains or hills? Are you in a valley? Is there water nearby?

Then, you can look for the mouth of Chi and how it enters the front door of your property. Again, check this area for clutter, dirt, or debris that might be in this area and clear it away

Inside your property, take a good look at the entrance way. Is it orderly, clean, inviting? Does the door swing freely open or does it hit something? Are there paintings or other art? Mirrors? A window or door opposite the entrance door?

Stand back and gaze on the area with a discriminating eye and look for anything that could impede the flow of Chi in the entry way; this would prevent the energy from flowing through the home or building, and make it stagnate.

Notice, too, how the property looks and smells: is it bright and cheerful or dark and foreboding? Does it smell pleasant? Scent is a very important aspect in Feng Shui and smells most definitely impact your Chi and the Chi of your surroundings. Scent has a distinct link to one's subconscious and so operates on both the physical and the metaphysical levels.

As you continue to walk through your property, check on the kitchen area: do all the burners work on your stove? Is your kitchen easy to work in? Look at the other rooms, assessing their colors and whether any of them is in need of repainting. Also as you walk through the property, check for broken moldings, windows, or chipped paint. Do your windows need to be cleaned? Do you like your curtains or would you want new ones, or entirely different window treatments?

You might want to make a list about what repairs or changes you feel inspired to make.

Feng Shui suggests you take a look at the artwork in your home: not just paintings, but photographs, posters, sculptures, figurines and the like. What do these pieces mean to you?

For that matter, maybe it's time to do a 'floor shift' and move your furniture around. Sometimes, as you will see in the stories in this book, doing this not only refreshes the whole room, but 'finds' space you didn't know you had for something wonderful.

As you look around your home, also try to recall if there is a particular room that guests seem to gravitate to. Is one room more comfortable than another for some reason? You may want to try to figure out why this might be the case, and see if a change of paint, furniture placement or artwork would make the room more welcoming.

Finally, but very importantly, Feng Shui suggests you check out your bedroom. We spend more than a third of our life in our bedroom, so it is a very important place. Do you sleep well? Do you love the color of the bedroom? What about the décor? Are there mirrors in your bedroom? Is there a television there? Do you have a comfortable and supportive bed; is it yours or is it a hand me down? Open the closet doors and try to recall the last time they were cleaned out. Is the space under the bed clear, and clean?

This might seem like one unending series of questions, questions, questions, but this will stir your intuition and imagination into action. Asking yourself these questions and really taking the time to answer them will help you identify the areas you want to change in your home or office or other space, and see why making those changes will change your life. It will also enable you to reacquaint yourself with areas of your home or space and appreciate what you truly do love about it.

When we connect with our homes and living spaces in a way that feels supportive and comfortable, we are able to create a happy and harmonious environment. Our wish is for you to manifest lasting, positive and beneficial Chi in your life. With some of the examples cited in the stories as inspiration, and the text as a guide, we hope you will be able to enhance your aspirations and your well being. This will lead to a happy and harmonious you, and have a home that feels truly welcoming.

"Welcome Home," will take on a whole new meaning.

Namaste!

ABOUT THE AUTHORS

Sybilla R. Lenz has worked as a Feng Shui consultant for 12 years. She is certified in both BTB and Classical Feng Shui. Lenz has been a financial and insurance professional for more than 20 years, helping people accumulate and manage their assets; she has her own business in northeastern Pennsylvania.

Deborah Courville has worked as a journalist for more than 20 years, and is also the author of a number of popular fiction books. She holds a B.A. in Theology and an M.A. in English. Feng Shui has assisted her in obtaining the tools to create the life she has always wanted.

Both Lenz and Courville live in rural northeastern Pennsylvania.

Contact the authors at
welcomehomebalboa2012@hotmail.com.

RESOURCES

Hale, Gill (2003), The Practical Encyclopedia of Feng Shui, Anness Publishing, Ltd.

Kunders, G.D. (2011), Designing Hospitals of the Future, Prism Books

Lenz, Sybilla R. (2008), The Energy Atlas (DVD), The Authoring House at DiscMakers

www.positivelivingfengshui.com

REFERENCES

Hale, Gill (2003), The Practical Encyclopedia of Feng Shui, Anness Publishing, Ltd.

Kunders, G.D. (2011), Designing Hospitals of the Future, Prism Books

McTaggert, Lynne (2008), The Intention Experiment, Free Press/Simon and Schuster

Santopietro, Nancy (2002), Feng Shui and Health, Three Rivers Press